WIT
SILVER L⎯⎯⎯

By

Allan P McLean

Illustrated by John Mackay

C000069193

"Mary Queen of Scots" was published in 1987 by Lang Syne Publishing, Old School, Blanefield, Glasgow, and printed by Waterside Printers. © Langsyne Publishing. ISBN 1 85217 100 6.

"Without a knowledge of the legend and romance of any nation, we cannot adequately apprehend the essential characteristics which distinguish it from every other."

— *P. Hume Brown, M.A., LL.D., Historiographer-Royal for Scotland, 1907.*

For my daughter Helen, who loves castles

MARY OF GUISE

KING JAMES V

MARY QUEEN OF SCOTS

KING JAMES VI

5

LORD DARNLEY   FALKLAND PALACE

PALACE OF HOLYROODHOUSE

6

MARY QUEEN OF SCOTS HOUSE,   EDINBURGH CASTLE
JEDBURGH   FROM THE GRASSMARKET

LINLITHGOW PALACE

LOCH LEVEN CASTLE   NIDDRY CASTLE

CRAIGMILLAR CASTLE, EDINBURGH

8

TANTALLON CASTLE AND BASS ROCK

TRAQUHAIR HOUSE

9

BORTHWICK CASTLE　　　　CRICHTON CASTLE

ST. ANDREWS CASTLE

BLAIR CASTLE   HAILES CASTLE

INCHMAHOME PRIORY

11

DUNDRENNON ABBEY

HERMITAGE CASTLE

Introduction

*O*ur story begins at two palaces. The walls of one bear mute witness to the last gasps of a dying man. The stones of the other echo to the cries of a new-born babe.

It is December, 1542. The maternity palace is at Linlithgow, 18 miles west of Edinburgh. The baby is days away from becoming Queen. Nobody knows it yet, but she is to be one of the most romantic and most hauntingly tragic figures in history, Mary Queen of Scots.

The other palace is away to the north of the Firth of Forth, at Falkland, where Mary's father King James V has gone to die. His soldiers have been routed by the English at Solway Moss, one of Scotland's most shameful defeats in battle.

In the midst of his sorrow news is brought of the birth at Linlithgow. He has had sons by his mistresses, but they cannot inherit the throne. His wife bore him two sons, but they died in infancy.

Another legitimate son, strong and healthy, is what the king most craves. He is told that he has fathered a daughter. His last words on this earth are a melancholy forecast of doom. He turns his face to the wall and dies.

Chapter One

That Sweet Face

*T*he journalists on their way to see Pope John Paul were surprised to meet the Rev Ian Paisley.

He stepped out of a car in Edinburgh's Royal Mile beside St Giles Cathedral, the High Kirk where more than 400 years before the great Protestant John Knox had preached against the Roman Catholic religion of Mary Queen of Scots.

The reporters were waiting at a pre-arranged pick-up point for a private bus to go through the tight security around St Mary's Cathedral where the Pope was about to attend a service for nuns and monks. The Democratic Unionist MP had arrived coincidentally to show some Ulster friends the site of John Knox's grave. They were in Edinburgh to commemorate the Scottish Protestant Martyrs, a subject on which Mr Paisley is an enthusiastic expert.

Not wanting to miss the opportunity of a story the newspapermen spent the remaining minutes before the arrival of the papal visit bus in the company of the big man from Ulster. He pointed out the exact spot where the mortal remains of Knox lie buried, where the leading lights of the Scottish legal system now park their cars when attending the Court of Session and the High Court.

Then, on that unique evening in May, 1982, it was off down the Royal Mile on the circuitous route insisted upon by the police to avoid roads which were closed to traffic temporarily for the first visit of a reigning Pope to Scotland. The bus went past the site of the grim house where Mary Queen of Scots was held prisoner amid scenes of mayhem in the street in 1567, on by John Knox's House, and round the quaint little stone building known charmingly but inaccurately to generations of Edinburgh folk as Queen Mary's Bath House, near her Palace of Holyroodhouse.

Such had been the strength of the reformed religion that ousted Roman Catholicism in Scotland during Mary's time that a papal visit would have been inconceivable throughout most of the four centuries since. But these days the Roman Catholic Church in Scotland and the Church of Scotland issue joint Press releases, and it had already been accepted before that occasion in 1982 that the Moderator of the General Assembly of the Church of Scotland could meet the Pope — although there are still those who hold it to be controversial.

Issues dating back to Mary's reign surfaced in heated debate in Edinburgh in May, 1986, when the Westminster Confession of Faith was spoken of at the General Assembly of the Church of Scotland, and also across the Royal Mile at the General Assembly of the Free Church of Scotland, which had broken away over fundamental disagreements in 1843.

The confession, adopted at the time of the Reformation in Scotland in 1560, still represents the basis of belief for members of both these churches, the Kirk and the Free Kirk. But a Kirk elder complained that he was unable to accept some parts which may have been right for the sixteenth century, but which in the changed times of the twentieth were just offensive to Roman Catholics with whom Kirk members work as Christian friends.

The Assembly agreed that it is possible to be an elder of the Kirk today without having to regard the Pope as the Anti-Christ. Presbyterians who no longer saw similarities between Satanism and Roman Catholicism ruled the day, in a spirit of conciliation which would surely have been approved of by Mary, who was the Catholic queen of a Protestant country.

During her reign she was tolerant of the new religion, and wished tolerance for hers in return. Her toleration was more in keeping with our own time than hers. But echoes of the angry confrontations which ex-

16

ercised Queen Mary's Scots are still to be heard. While the Kirk Assembly was deliberating in 1986, the General Assembly of the Free Kirk was hearing a vigorous defence of the Westminster Confession in all its fiery detail from their Moderator

The papal visit and these Church debates were not the only events of the 1980s to throw up reminders of Mary Queen of Scots and the Scotland of her reign. On a rainswept Edinburgh morning in July, 1986, police motorcyclists coasted down St Mary's Street, in a move which attracted the attention of people sheltering in doorways round about. They rushed forward into the rain to see who was being escorted. "It's Diana!" a man shouted, and there was a spontaneous outbreak of waving.

As the black limousine glided past, following the line of the Flodden Wall built to protect Scotland's capital after that defeat of 1513, the Princess of Wales smiled and waved back. The sudden glimpse of her famous face brought Mary Queen of Scots to mind. She, too, was tall, beautiful and much admired, and it suddenly struck me that the Princess of Wales, who has brought an additional link with the Stuarts to the Royal family, has attractive features remarkably similar to those of Mary, particularly her distinctive nose, so characteristic of the Stuarts.

It may be four centuries since Mary Stuart met her death, but she is still capable of being regarded as dangerous. Or at least that is what the Post Office seems to think. Notorious for ignoring events of Scottish interest when issuing special commemorative stamps, the British postal authorities came up with a novel excuse for missing the 400th anniversary of Queen Mary.

"The character and story of Mary Queen of Scots still arouses religious controversy", a spokesman for the Post Office Board said, when asked about the decision. That a British Government department, backed by the Scottish Post Office Board, had come up with the idea of a Queen Mary stamp in the first place cut no ice with the national postal authority for the UK.

HM Historiographer for Scotland, Profesor Gordon Donaldson, commented to a reporter: "The Post Office appears to be taking the English point of view that the proper thing to do with Queen Mary was to chop off her head .... In fact, the Queen today is descended from Mary Stuart and not from Elizabeth who was rightly called the Virgin Queen and died childless. English people are not aware of this fact and it is difficult to convince them of it."

But enough of these thoughts from the 1980s! It is time to look back to the Scotland of Mary Stuart, and then learn something of her too brief life before visiting a selection of the buildings associated with the queen whose arrival in Edinburgh in 1561 caused the people to shout: "Heaven bless that sweet face!"

Chapter Two

A Parcel of Rogues

Scotland had an abiding problem in the sixteenth century, as in so many other periods. It was money, or rather, the lack of it.

In Queen Mary's time the national economy was in such a bad way that the value of Scottish money was halved between 1544 and 1565.

There was never enough of the stuff for royalty to rule the place properly. There was never enough to keep all the grasping nobles happy. On occasions, Scottish monarchs were known to pawn some of their jewellery — otherwise the licentious, unpaid, unfed soldiery might have turned rather nastier than usual. As it was the Scottish armies had a tendency to thin out a bit around harvest time, as the troops slipped away home to reap their vital food supplies.

Sometimes, too, their leaders could prove a rum lot, holding back from attack at crucial times when confronted by the English. Money might have had something to do with that, too.

In his song "Fareweel To A' Our Scottish Fame" Robert Burns damned the Scots commissioners — equivalent to MPs — who agreed to the Treaty of Union with England which abolished Scotland's Parliament in 1707. He accused "a coward few" of selling their country for English bribes, "hireling traitors' wages".

The final angry couplet of his song could just as well have applied in previous centuries:

We're bought and sold for English gold;
Such a parcel of rogues in a nation!

The allocation of silver with which to sweeten Scottish nobles had been a standard part of the

English government's budget for many a year. Doling out cash to leading lights of the Scottish community was no eighteenth century wheeze on the part of scheming neighbours on the southern side of the Border; it was established long before.

It was a vital part of English foreign policy to give valuable gifts to selected representatives of the only independent nation to continue to menace England from another part of the same island. The Channel might help deter the French from invading, but, the English reasoning went, the Scots had to be bought, except when they were being treated to a bout of periodic English violence.

When Scottish nobles were captured in battle and taken south as prisoners they would often be offered their freedom, and a sufficiency of silver, in return for promising to attend to English interests after going home to Scotland. In her definitive history of *Mary* Queen of Scots (Weidenfield and Nicholson), Lady An tonia Fraser likens these gentlemen to so many Trojan horses. (It has to be said that some took the English money, but then supported Scottish interests on their return.)

Mary was to face disastrous problems because of the tendency of the Scottish aristocracy to look after themselves without too much concern for the nation. For too long Scottish kings had come to the throne as children, leaving the country inevitably open to feuding rivals. The coronation of the baby girl once again left poor, vulnerable Scotland in the invidious position it had suffered so often.

Possession of the king's person was a handy way to make sure your interests prevailed, and frequently one rival faction or another would seek to take custody of the child king and then issue proclamations in his name. This was a fate that was to befall Mary's son King James VI, who went on to become James I of England, and there were to be some distinctly nasty recriminations once the king was free.

Possession of the queen's person could be considered a whole lot more interesting than holding a king, particularly when the queen had grown to be an attractive young woman. But that's something we will come to later. As a child, she was the object of political interest, the argument being whether she was to be cared for in England, France, or Scotland.

Looking back with twentieth century eyes, sixteenth century Scotland seems a violent and dangerous place, but it is worth remembering that the atrocities of our own age in so many parts of the world are on a far larger scale of horror.

Most of the 700,000 population of Scotland 400 years ago were illiterate peasants whose lives were frequently at risk from disease and starvation. There were brilliant intellectuals among the country's leaders (although even some aristocrats were illiterate and many seem to have been uncouth and notoriously unclean, baths being thought of as unhealthy). There were extremes of wealth and poverty.

The ladies at Queen Mary's court may have been dressed in velvet robes, draped with gold chains, with a life of frivolity, sweet music and gentle dancing, but for most women life was summed up by the apt old Scots expression: "a sair fecht." Dresses were loose garments of the simplest kind, and shoes were a luxury. The peasants worked hard, lived with cattle in smokey hovels and died young.

Even the nobles were unable to escape from the terrible diseases of the time, and the wives of the aristocrats were as likely to die in childbirth as anyone else. For the peasants many children were necessary, to ensure that enough survived to become adults who could work to look after their parents, if they lived long enough themselves. For the nobility, there was also a likelihood that many children would fail to grow up and sons were needed to protect the interests of property. This led to a quaint Scottish custom whereby a man and woman would live together as man-and-wife for a year. If at the end of that time there was no bairn on the way the "handfast marriage" was over and they were each free to find another partner who might have a better prospect of parenthood.

21

At a time when death was perhaps the most obvious fact of life, it was little wonder that religion was considered to be important, as in many Third World countries today. But the Church was in no fit state to give the spiritual guidance the people craved, the abbots and bishops enjoying immense wealth, which brought with it good food, fine clothes, and comfortable beds in which to dally with mistresses. In spite of the vow of chastity, Church leaders fathered illegitimate children and then used influence to get land, titles and power for these offspring of supposedly celibate fathers.

There were moves within the Church to gain reform including attempts to ensure that the parishes had the services of priests who could read, write and preach. Too many, it seems, were pathetic souls who were just not up to the task. Obviously there were others who upheld the values of their religion, but those who wished to reform the Church and maintain the historic link with Rome were fighting a losing battle in Scotland. The call for a reformed Church of Scotland owing no allegiance to the Pope became a truly popular one at all levels of society.

Support by the aristocrats no doubt contained elements of self-interest. The Church was immensely wealthy before the Reformation but poor after it, new hands having acquired the land. In 1556 Cardinal Sermoneta wrote to the Pope that the Church in Scotland "far surpassed the laity in the wealth and substance of its resources." And yet one of the tasks Mary Stuart had to tackle in the 1560s was the need to provide an income for the impoverished ministers of the Reformed Church.

The moral argument for reform won the day, helped, too, by the printed word. Few could read or write, but their numbers were growing, breaking the old virtual monopoly of the Church in literacy. The old need for monks to copy books by hand was overtaken by printing. Initially Bibles — in English rather than Scots — were imported from Europe. The spread of readers followed the setting up of Scotland's first printing press in Edinburgh by Walter Chapman and Androw Myllar during the reign of Mary's grandfather, King James IV.

In their drive to maintain public order and morals the reformers sought to stamp out some of Scotland's traditional fun-and-games, including the Mayday Robin Hood celebrations during which some licence had been given to the Abbot of Unreason. The habit of plying funeral mourners and wedding guests with vast quantities of drink was also frowned upon, because poor people often felt obliged to spend money they were unable to afford and the reformers were genuinely concerned for the wellbeing of the people.

English interests, certainly after 1558, were keen to see Kirk reform in Scotland, as this was a way to cut Scotland off from the Auld Alliance with Catholic France. There were still many Catholics around, but the Protestant view prevailed. The Church of Scotland held its first General Assembly in 1560. The arguments were based on moral principle, but force played a part, too, religious controversy provoking violence in the sixteenth as in other centuries.

"Bloody Mary" Tudor, Queen of England from 1553 to 1558, and wife of Philip II of Spain, gained her nickname from her thirst for having Protestants put to death. In France during the horrific St Bartholomew's Day Massacre in 1572 there was wholesale butchery of the French Protestants, the Huguenots.

And in Scotland, too, religion was a reason for violent death. George Wishart, the prominent preacher of the reformed faith whose words won the heart of John Knox, was widely regarded as a good and honest man. This displeased Cardinal David Beaton who ordered that Wishart should be burned at the stake at St Andrews in 1546. Three months later Beaton was dragged from the bed he shared with his mistress and hacked to death in revenge for his execution of the Protestant martyr. Beaton's French allies then took their revenge in turn, attacking St Andrews and making off with a number of Protestants, most notably John Knox, who was to spend 19 months as a galley slave of the French.

Violence was a common punishment for criminal as well as religious offences. Public executions were frequent, and for those for whom the penalty fell short of death there were such charming punishments as branding and the cutting off of ears. As well as wars between Scotland and England, there were English pirates to contend with who would slip out of East coast ports and capture Scottish merchant ships and their cargoes on the regular trade routes to France and other parts of Europe.

Nevertheless, the causes of peace and learning did move ahead during a period which saw the establishment in 1583 of Edinburgh University. Scotland's three other universities of the time had come into being at St Andrews, Glasgow and Aberdeen in the previous century, although after Edinburgh there was to be no other new university in Scotland until Strathclyde in 1964.

Chapter Three

Some Enchantment

"*I*t cam wi' a lass and it will gang wi' a lass", is said to be the reaction of King James V on hearing that his French wife, Mary of Guise, had borne a daughter.

In this he was both right and wrong. Right in that the Stuart dynasty was to be last represented on a throne by a reigning queen, wrong in thinking that it would be his baby girl who would end the line. His comment was a reference to Robert the Bruce's daughter Marjorie inaugurating the Stuarts as a result of her marriage to Walter, the Steward of Scotland. Their son Robert II came to the throne in 1371, the name Steward changing to Stewart and later Stuart.

The Stuarts' hold on the thrones of Scotland and then England ended with the death of Queen Anne in 1714. There is still Stuart blood in the British royal family. (The section of the Stuarts associated with Bonnie Prince Charlie were pushed out of the succession when King James VII of Scotland, II of England, was deposed in 1688 after attempting to restore Catholicism.)

But James V was certainly right to forecast trouble. The dynasty had known plenty. James I was assassinated at Perth in 1437 after angering his nobles by attempting to form a strong central government. James II established his authority after a long struggle but was killed by an exploding cannon as he besieged the English at Roxburgh in 1460. James III was murdered when he fled the battle field at Sauchieburn in 1488 after being defeated by his own nobles.

James IV seemed to make a better fist of it and even married Margaret Tudor, sister of Henry VIII, in an attempt to keep the peace with England. This marriage established the link which allowed Mary to claim the throne of England and eventually sent her son James VI to rule in London, but it failed to prevent war and James IV was killed in battle with the English at Flodden in 1513.

All this woe must have been in the mind of James V after the rout of Solway Moss on November 24, 1542. He took one of the fits of melancholy the Stuarts were heir to and retired to Falkland Palace. Mary was born at Linlithgow on December 8, and her father died six days later. He was just 31.

It might have been expected that Henry VIII would press home the advantage of Scotland's parlous state after the Solway Moss defeat and the premature death of her king, but the fearsome English ruler was superstitious and preferred a temporary peace to continuing with war so close upon the death of a monarch.

In the meantime, Henry sought other ways to establish England's centuries-old dream to dominate Scotland. There were rumours that the infant Queen was unwell, and might even be dead. If she lived Henry had a notion that she might come in handy. He offered English protection for the vulnerable baby, although it was not her interests he had in mind.

To reassure Henry about the baby Queen's health, and gender, she was displayed naked to the English ambassador, Sir Ralph Sadler, who found her as goodly a child as he had seen of that age "and as like to live, with the Grace of God."

In our day, the last thought anyone would be likely to entertain about a baby girl would be who she should marry. But a husband for Mary was already on the agenda even before she was weaned. Royal marriages were affairs of state, and it mattered not one whit that prospective partners were but children.

She should marry a Scot, some said. No! An Englishman should be her groom, came another view. And there is no need to guess the nationality of the prospective spouse to be favoured by France.

If Mary married a Scot, this would strengthen the family she married into, much to the chagrin of the other feuding families. James Hamilton, Earl of Arran, succeded in making himself governor of Scotland. As Regent his role was to run the country for the infant monarch, and the notion that struck him as a good one was that Mary should marry his son.

However, those Trojan horses in the form of Scottish nobility captured at Solway Moss were on their way home, released by Henry VIII after agreeing that an awfully nice idea would be for Mary to marry his son, Prince Edward, when she was 11 years old. Until then there would be peace between England and Scotland. The weak Arran was persuaded to go along with this line, which was agreed by the Treaty of Greenwich on July 1, 1543.

French and Catholic interests were not prepared to buy that one. Cardinal David Beaton, Archbishop of St Andrews, who had played a key role in bringing Mary of Guise to Scotland, mustered his forces and had the baby crowned at Stirling, where she had been taken to the castle as a place of safety. Beaton feared that the English might have made off with her from the insecurity of Linlithgow.

Henry VIII was not best pleased. After all hadn't he offered Arran an alternative daughter-in-law? All right so it was Elizabeth, Henry's daughter by Anne Boleyn. And Elizabeth had been declared illegitimate and had little prospect — so it seemed then — of ever coming to the throne of England. But she had royal English blood to match the royal Scottish blood of Arran's family, the Hamiltons.

Arran became a Catholic on September 8, 1543, and the very next day took part in the coronation of the baby Mary at Stirling Castle; it was the thirtieth anniversary of the Battle of Flodden. Sir Ralph Sadler reported to Henry that the simple ceremony was of a kind favoured in Scotland — "not very costlie."

Henry was still anxious to pursue England's interests, but it was to prove increasingly difficult to keep control of those Scots he had sought to influence in his favour. What happened next was to receive one of those charming titles accorded to various episodes in Scottish history in a way that showed a sense of humour in adversity. What Henry ordered came to be known as "the Rough Wooing". He had tried peaceful means to have his way, but in December, 1543, Scotland decided to renew its association with France in the "Auld Alliance" against the country still known today to Scottish football supporters as the "Auld Enemy" — England. The team Henry mustered under the Earl of Hertford to teach the Scots a lesson and win them by force was a decidedly rougher crew than the chaps in white shirts who have visited Hampden in our own time.

The evil side of the English king is well known thanks to his attitude to his wives. It is also shown in his orders to Hertford for the Rough Wooing. Edinburgh and Leith were to be burned and defaced to leave a memory of the vengeance forever. In towns and villages around no stone was to be left standing. Hertford's men were to put "man, woman and child to the sword without exception where any resistance is made". Cardinal Beaton and the Regent Arran had got wind of what was about to happen, but too late to prepare effective resistance.

On the afternoon of Saturday, May 4, 1544, the 200 ships bearing proud King Henry's men arrived off Leith. Next morning they came ashore, brushing the Scots forces aside at Wardie and beside the Water of Leith before moving in on the port, which was stoutly defended. But after much fighting, Leith fell, and England's ships could find safe haven. For a week the English looted and destroyed, taking booty which they said represented a far greater amount of wealth than they would have expected to find in a Scottish town. Edinburgh was put to the torch, blazing for three days and nights. All around, destruction was visited upon the smallest cottage and in the Firth of Forth ships were attacked.

Henry was ecstatic when he read Hertford's account of how the English leaders stood upon Calton Hill and admired the fires around them, delighting in the horrified screams of anguish from women and children. After finally destroying the last of Leith by fire, the English set off home by land, pillaging as they went. Their ships were so heavily laden with stolen goods that they were unable to take all the troops they had brought.

Many of the inhabitants of Edinburgh, Holyrood and Leith had escaped before the arrival of the English. The people came out of hiding in the marshy country nearby to find their homes gone.

Henry's ships were later busy in war with France, giving the desperate merchants of Edinburgh and Leith the chance to recoup at least some of their losses by sending ships down the East coast of England to raid vessels which were trading in and out of Newcastle, Hull, Yarmouth and other ports. The English concentration in the Channel meant there was no resistance.

In 1547 Henry died of "the French disease" and King Francis I of France died of "la Maladie Anglaise." In spite of each country thus labelling the illness as the fault of the other, it was the same disease — syphillis, which was much more virulent then than it is now. At that stage the policies of England remained as before and Scotland was set for another dire event — Black Saturday.

This time the English forces came by land and on September 10, 1547, Scotland suffered defeat at the Battle of Pinkie, near Musselburgh, on the approach to Edinburgh. Pinkie Cleuch left 400 Scots widows, whose husbands became known as "the sons of heroes slain at Flodden". Next day when the men led by Hertford, now the Duke of Somerset, marched along the shore at Leith they found the port "all desolate, for not a soul did we find in the town." With the previous looting in mind, the people had upped and gone during the night, taking their valuables with them. The house of John Barton was set alight. He was one of Leith's heroic seamen, from the family of "fighting Bartons" who had gained notoriety among the English for attacks on that country's shipping. Then the rest of Leith was burned again and the English set off by land

and sea for home, leaving garrisons behind on the Forth islands of Inchkeith and Inchcolm.

All this while the little Queen Mary had been growing up at Stirling, but the defeat at Pinkie led to fears that the English might even be able to kidnap her from that stronghold, in spite of the castle, like that at Edinburgh, having an air of impregnability from its post atop a rock.

For a time she was spirited away from Stirling Castle to be cared for by the monks on an island in the middle of a loch which also has as a claim to fame the fact that it isn't. It's a lake, the Lake of Menteith, where the ruins of Mary's shelter at Inchmahome Priory still stand and there's a nice little story about her garden. Robert the Bruce had hidden there

I am unsure which garden was the one in the nursery rhyme, but she already had four childhood companions who feature in that rhyme, and don't in another although people think they do! These were the four Maries, so known not just because they were all called Mary but because Marie was the term given to a maid of honour. There have been suggestions that there may have been five or even six Maries, but that is possibly explained by attempts to account for a mistake by Sir Walter Scott. The four Maries who were to accompany Mary for a large part of her life were Mary Fleming, whose mother was an illegitimate daughter of James IV, Mary Beaton, one of the Cardinal's family, Mary Seton, of the family whose East Lothian home was later a favourite haunt of the Queen and whose West Lothian home was to be a place of refuge for her, and Mary Livingston, daughter of Lord Livingston.

Mary Fleming's mother, Janet Stewart, Lady Fleming, was one of the Pinkie widows. She was the girls' governess.

Sir Walter Scott, not to mention my mother's teacher in Morayshire 70 years ago, thought the Queen's Maries were described in this verse:

Yestreen the Queen had four Maries

Tonight there'll be but three:
There's Mary Seton and Mary Beaton
And Mary Carmichael and me.

I am indebted to Lady Antonia Fraser's biography of the Queen for tracing this to a scandal with Scottish links at the court of Tsar Peter the Great in Russia in the early eighteenth century, when one Mary Hamilton was executed for the murder of a child. The Queen of Scots was served by no Mary Carmichael.

It is the nursery rhyme that refers to Mary Stuart, the cockle shells being mementoes worn by pilgrims, the bells being used in Mass, and the four Maries being the pretty maids. Like many nursery rhymes it began as political satire:

Mary, Mary quite contrary
How does your garden grow?
With cockle shells, and silver bells,
And pretty maids all in a row.

Scotland had become too dangerous for Mary, not yet six years old. On July 7, 1548, with the pro-French faction holding the upper hand, it was agreed that she should marry the Dauphin Francis, the sickly wee lad who was destined to be King of France. The English pirates left behind on the Forth islands made an East coast escape unwise, so it was decided to take Mary, her four Maries, their governess and leading Scottish figures on a Western route from Dumbarton Castle on the Clyde. The little Queen took her leave of her mother, the Dowager Queen Mary, and set sail on August 7, 1548.

The party had been aboard ship waiting for good sailing weather for a few days before finally leaving the Clyde. Lady Fleming did not take kindly to the sea and asked to be put ashore, only to be told by the captain that she would go to France and like it, or drown. Mary, however, seems to have found delight in the voyage, it being reported back to her mother that the cheeky wee lass made fun of those of her company who were sea sick.

Arrival at Roscoff on August 13 was to bring new

31

adulation for Mary, from the crowds who welcomed her with rapturous cries of "Vive la Reinette!" (Long Live the Little Queen!). Her older Stewart half-brothers, James, Robert and John, who are understood to have been in the party, doubtless felt jealous.

Illustration 1 — Mary as a young girl in France, with her mother Mary of Guise and a lute player.

Her years in France were to be a largely happy time, in spite of a plot to poison her in 1551, occasional bouts of toothache and several illnesses. To be ill was no surprise in those days, but survival was never certain, so her health was a topic of great concern. She was fortunate in the French physician who cared for her around 1557 when she suffered from smallpox because he had a special treatment which appears to have been successful in protecting her beautiful complexion from permanent damage.

It might be expected that fawning courtiers would constantly say nice things about the wee Queen, but there is no doubt that she was truly attractive, even though the poet Pierre Brantôme might be thought to be going just a little over the top when he wrote: "... as her youth grew on, we saw her great beauty and her great virtues grow likewise; so that, coming to her fifteenth year, her beauty shone like the light at mid-day ..."

Certainly there are portraits of her around which fail to capture much sign of beauty, but these artless apparitions were fashioned by those who never saw her, and at best were based on the view of her after years of illegal captivity in England. Those who saw her in life, especially as a girl and young woman, were much taken by her appearance and her personality. Even John Knox took note.

King Henry of France is said to have remarked on first seeing the young Mary: "This is the most perfect child I have ever seen."

At that time she was described by her grandmother, the Duchess de Guise, thus: "She is *brune*, with a clear complexion, and I think that she will be a beautiful girl, for her complexion is fine and clear, the skin white, the lower part of the face very pretty, the eyes are small and rather deep set, the face rather long, she is graceful and not shy, on the whole we may well be contented with her."

Her appearance as a young woman at her most attractive is probably best caught in two real works of art done from life at the French court. One is the famous crayon sketch by the court painter, Francois Clouet. The other is a bronze bust by Jacquio Ponce, made in 1559 or 1560, and purchased in 1982 by the Scottish National Portrait Gallery in Queen Street, Edinburgh.

33

She wears the French Imperial Crown, decorated with the fleur-de-lys, and in spite of the intervention of four centuries and the cold, hard nature of the metal, the radiant beauty of the subject is obvious.

In 1906 Andrew Lang complained in his book *"Portraits and Jewels of Mary Stuart"* (published in Glasgow by James MacLehose & Sons) about "pseudo Maries" purported to be the Queen. Of portraits at the Glasgow International Exhibition of 1901 "she in no way resembled 15 out of the 18 portraits exhibited for public edification."

Lang continued: "One thing is historically certain: Mary was either beautiful, or she bewitched people into thinking her beautiful. This is proved, not by the eulogies of Ronsard and Brantôme, a courtly poet, and a courtly chronicler, but by the unanimous verdict of friend and enemy. Even Knox calls her face 'pleasing' — which the authentic portraits of her face hardly ever are: even Elizabeth recognised something 'divine' in her hated rival; Sir James Melville styles her 'very loesome'; the populace of Edinburgh cried: 'Heaven bless that sweet face', says Knox, as she rode by, while English and French ambassadors are in the same tale."

He also quoted: "There is some enchantment by which men are bewitched", adding: "and 'bewitched' more than a married man ought to be, was Ruthven by Mary, when she lay captive in Loch Leven Castle (1567)."

Lang concluded: "What stood between the artists and her beauty? Their own limitations supply the answer."

Chapter Four

No Judge of Men

*I*t was in France that her beauty flowered. So did her intellect. As well as the expected womanly pursuit of embroidery, and the development of her talent for music, Mary was given an education fit for the crowned queen of one realm and the future queen of another. It was unfortunate, perhaps, that she gained her knowledge of statecraft in the mollycoddling surroundings of the French court where she learned that family members supported each other and her de Guise relations were to be trusted. The treacherous rough-and-tumble of Scotland was to be so different, and she was unprepared for the slow and painful discovery that her Scottish relatives, never mind apparent friends, could be trusted only to look after their personal aggrandizement, regardless of supposed loyalty.

But nevertheless, as she grew up in France those who met her were struck by her educated ability to reason, as well as her engaging personality and spectacular beauty. As a later inventory of her library in Edinburgh was to show, she was an avaricious reader. As well as her native Scots tongue, she became fluent in French, a language she was to use in writing many letters over the years. She must have had a facility for languages, as she learned Latin, Italian and Spanish, too, and seems to have acquired at least some Greek as books in this language were included in her library. But she never learned English until her captivity in that land.

Incidentally, if poor Scotland was looked down

35

upon by the English, it was a tendency shared by at least some in France. Brantôme shows prejudice against Scottish people, language and clothing in these descriptions of Mary:

"At all times when she talked with others she used a most gentle, dainty, agreeable style of speech, with kindly majesty, mingled, however, with discreet and modest reserve, and above all with beautiful grace; so that even her native tongue, which in itself is very rustic, barbarous, ill-sounding, and uncouth, she spoke so gracefully, toning it in such a way that she made it seem beautiful and agreeable in her, though never so in others."

And:

"See what virtue there was in such beauty and grace that they could turn coarse barbarism into sweet civility and social grace. We must not be surprised therefore that being dressed (as I have seen her) in the barbarous costume of the uncivilised people of her country, she appeared, in mortal body and coarse ungainly clothing a true goddess .... She had also one other perfection with which to charm the world — a voice most sweet and excellent; for she sang well, at-tuning her voice to the lute, which she touched very prettily with that white hand and those fingers, perfect-ly made ...."

She also used those fingers to write a constant stream of letters to her mother in Scotland, where the Queen Dowager continued to live whatever Brantôme may have thought of the uncivilised, coarse barbarity of the place. The signature on the letters home was to remain Mary's standard autograph on all cor-respondence for the rest of her life: "marie", each let-ter formed to the same height.

There is no doubt that both mother and daughter grieved their separation, but Mary of Guise had to look after her daughter's interests in Scotland. The Queen Dowager became Regent in 1554, succeeding the inef-fective Arran, who now had a French title — Duke of Châtelherault. When Mary was almost eight years old her mother paid her a visit in France, but it was the last time they met. On receiving news that her mother was to come, Mary wrote that it gave her "the greatest happiness which I could wish for in this world." Their parting was tearful, and when the 17-year-old Mary heard nine years later that her mother was ill, the young Queen took to her bed.

Mary of Guise died at Edinburgh Castle on June 11, 1560, after being ill for some time with dropsy. John Knox saw the hand of God in this fatal illness which made "her belly and loathsome legs to swell". The news reached France on June 18, but it was another 10 days before anyone dared tell Mary. She collapsed in dreadful grief, the Venetian ambassador noting that Mary loved her mother much more than daughters usually love their mothers.

Another event which had marred Mary's time in France was when her governess, Lady Fleming, was sent home in disgrace. She had become pregnant by King Henry II. This caused annoyance at court, partly because Lady Fleming went around boasting about her affair with the King and the fruitful result, but also because she had disturbed the tranquility of the charming *ménage à trois*, involving the King, his mistress, Diane de Poitiers, and his wife, Queen Catherine de Medicis. Queen Catherine was prepared to tolerate Diane, whose colours were sported by the King with the letters D and H entwined, but the intervention of the indiscreet Lady Fleming was too much.

But there were many happy times, too, as the court moved from one grand château such as Fontainebleau, Blois and Chambord to another. These castles, even in the sixteenth century, were much more comfortable than the forbidding establishments Mary was to find on her return to Scotland, in spite of French influence being apparent in the architecture at Falkland, Linlithgow and Stirling. It is said that Mary's favourite château was at Anet, built for Diane de Poitiers.

Ever since her arrival in France Mary was constantly in the company of the Dauphin, Francis. This fragile wee lad was constantly ill and the child Queen was encouraged to shower affection on the invalid. When Mary was 15 and Francis was 14 it was decided that they should marry, thus strengthening links between France and Scotland against England and satisfying the ambitions of Mary's uncles, the Duke de Guise and Cardinal de Guise, in boosting the power of their family.

Among the Scots Commissioners who came to negotiate the marriage contract was James Stewart, Mary's half-brother who was believed to think that he should have been King of Scotland. His father, after all, was King James V and it was just an inconvenience that the parents were not married to each other.

Like any royal marriage of the day, it was arranged for political reasons, but in this case the young couple do seem to have been in love, even if the affection was born from their being brought up together.

A public marriage document signed by Mary guaranteed the independence of Scotland, to the satisfaction of the Scottish Commissioners. The ancient freedoms of the nation were to be protected. As long as Mary was abroad, the Queen Mother would continue as Regent and if Mary died without children the Scottish throne would go to the nearest heir by blood, at that time the Duke of Châtelherault, the head of the Hamiltons.

But secret documents were also drawn up and signed by Mary. If she died childless Scotland would pass to France, and Mary's claim to the throne of England would be awarded to the French crown. The Scottish revenues were to be paid to the King of France until he recovered money spent in defence of Scotland. Mary was also persuaded to renounce in advance any later agreement which might contradict these secret pledges, which if put into effect would leave Scotland firmly under the thumb of France.

The marriage took place amid splendour on April 24, 1558, at the Cathedral of Notre Dame in Paris. There was a huge decorated canopy outside and decoration inside the cathedral included a giant bridal arch. Royalty, secular and church leaders graced the wedding procession, accompanied by brightly dressed musicians. Mary wore a luxurious white dress, diamonds sparkling around her, and a golden crown embellished with precious stones. In a gesture still echoed today in the Scottish tradition of the "pour-oot" in which coins are thrown to children, heralds went around shouting "Largesse! Largesse!" and tossing gold and silver to the crowd.

A lavish banquet followed, at which the jewel-encrusted crown became too heavy for Mary, and two men had to stand beside her, holding the crown above her head as she ate. Celebrations with expensively produced pageants went on for three days. Back home the Scots celebrated too, but a bit more cannily. Mons Meg, a huge, famous cannon, was fired from Edinburgh Castle battlements in salute. The cannonball landed two miles away on Wardie Muir, where a party of men was sent to bring it back to the castle!

In November, 1558, "Bloody Mary" Tudor of England died and her half-sister was declared Queen. But the view strongly promoted from France was that Elizabeth had no right to the throne of England, and Mary Stuart should be Queen of England instead. The young Mary was encouraged to regard herself the rightful heir to the English crown, an opinion which was later to be used against her. Elizabeth was the daughter of Henry VIII by Anne Boleyn, but in the opinion of the French, Henry VIII was still married to Catherine of Aragon at the time. This made Elizabeth illegitimate, the French argued. Henry VIII had contended that the marriage with Catherine of Aragon was invalid, but that cut no ice with the French who pointed out that Mary Stuart had descended in direct line from Henry VII, whose daughter Margaret Tudor had married King James IV of Scotland. According to the French, the only legitimate children of Henry VIII had been Mary Tudor by Catherine of Aragon and Edward VI by Jane Seymour, but neither left an heir. By 1559, with Spain allied to France through marriage instead of the previous connection between Spain and England, there was no way the English could accept a claim to their throne that added to the threat of hostility which surrounded England.

It is at this point that superstition enters the story, in the shape of an astrologer whose name is still regarded with awe in some quarters — Nostradamus. Queen Catherine de Medicis held him in high regard, and was alarmed when he begged her not to allow her husband Henry II to take risks. Nostradamus had a nasty dream. An old lion fought a young one and then rested before fighting a second time. In the new battle the young lion gouged the eye of the older one, which died from the wound. The old lion was identified as Henry II, whose death as a result of a duel was foretold by another astrologer.

The only problem with all this foretelling of doom, is that the French King paid no heed. Suitably garbed in his mistress's colours of black and white he decided he would indulge, regardless, in his favourite sport of jousting. After a bout with the Count of Montgomery, Henry challenged his opponent to a second contest. Montgomery begged to be excused, and Queen Catherine urged her husband to be content, and please not tempt fate.

Well, Henry was not the first husband to ignore his wife's advice, and he was not the last. And sure enough there was an accident. The young lion Montgomery struck the old lion Henry's helmet, raising the visor. A splinter from Montgomery's lance entered Henry's eye. It was only after 10 days' agonising pain that Henry died, his brain damaged by the splinter. He insisted on his death bed that Montgomery — a Protestant — was not to blame.

Mary Stuart, suddenly transmogrified from Dauphiness to Queen of France, wrote to her mother that Catherine "is plunged in such grief for the loss of the late King, that I fear her misery will give her a bad illness." Catherine vented that misery on the mistress, Diane, who was told to return the château at Chenonceaux which Henry had given her, and was presented with an inventory of jewels and other fancy presents donated by the late King. The items on this list were to be handed back, too. The entwined initials H and D were ingeniously reworked to become H and C. In place of Chenonceaux, Diane was given the château of Chaumont, which was regarded as an unlucky place.

On September 19, 1559, King Francis II was crowned at Rheims. It was said that France had three kings: Mary's husband Francis of Valois who wore the crown, Mary's uncle Francis de Guise who headed the army, and Mary's other uncle the Cardinal of Lorraine, heading the state. Catherine de Medicis obviously supported her son, and had no taste for the Guise ascendancy.

Francis continued in poor health, and there was a strong call for him to produce an heir. Sadly, it seems he suffered from undescended testicles, a complaint which prevented him being a father. Indeed, there is doubt as to whether Mary's first marriage was ever consummated. There is a suggestion that the Cardinal of Lorraine advised Mary to take a lover so that an heir could be assured, but whatever the young Queen's enemies were later to try and make of her reputation in Scotland, she never accepted this counsel, if it was ever given. Certainly the Guises were desperate for an heir, because if Francis died childless he would be succeeded by his ten-year-old brother Charles and Catherine would assume the role of power in the land.

Then came 1560, which was to prove to be a dreadfully distressing year for Mary Stuart. In June came the appalling news of her mother's death. By August the Protestant leaders, known as the Lords of the Congregation had won religious Reformation in Scotland, the Estates, the Scottish Parliament, approving the Confession of Faith, banning the Mass, and denying the authority of the Pope.

Meanwhile, the pathetically unhealthy Francis was suffering horribly from exceptionally painful headaches and sickness. Poor Mary was constantly by his side, desperately trying to nurse·him back to fitness. It was a losing battle. Inflammation from his ear spread steadily into his brain, where an abscess

41

formed. It was an agonising death. After he finally suc-
cumbed on December 5, Mary gave herself up to
boundless grief.

Speculation about a new husband had begun even
before Francis was dead, with echoes of the arguments
about a prospective spouse for Mary when she was still
a baby in Scotland 18 years before. Her Guise uncles
wanted her to marry her late husband's young brother
Charles IX. Catherine de Medicis opposed that notion.

Eric XIV of Sweden, Frederick II of Denmark and
the Earl of Arran thought themselves eligible. Henry,
Lord Darnley, offered the condolences of his mother,
but might have had marriage in mind even then.

The least charming groom on offer was Don
Carlos, son of Philip II of Spain. A small, wizened,
deformed lad, with one shoulder higher than the other,
and a speech impediment, Carlos was quite mad, a
problem not helped by an operation carried out on his
brain in an attempt to cure his partial paralysis. Philip
ruled out the match.

There was to be no second marriage yet. Sir
Nicholas Throckmorton, the English ambassador,
reported to Queen Elizabeth that the Queen of Scots
had taken on a new firmness of purpose since the
death of her husband. She showed great wisdom and
great judgment for her years, he declared. In view of
what was to happen later, it is interesting to note that
at this time Mary Stuart was regarded as an intelligent
ruler whereas Elizabeth Tudor was thought of as the
flighty one.

The Venetian ambassador remarked that Mary
had lost France and was uncertain of Scotland. She
had estates at Touraine and Poitou and might have
stayed on in France, but she no longer felt wanted
there. Scotland had become a Protestant land, and she
remained a devout Catholic. The French had become
unpopular in Scotland, where Mary was regarded as
French because she had spent most of her life in
France. However, she was the Queen of Scots and it
was to Scotland that she resolved to go.

In going there she was to place her trust in certain

42

men, and it might be thought in view of subsequent events that she was unwise in this. In this connection it is interesting to quote the opinion of Mary given in *"A History of Scotland"* (Methuen & Co) by Rosalind Mitchison: "She was undersexed, athletic, something of a tomboy, and of absolute physical courage. She did not shirk battle, actual or diplomatic, but she had a distaste for ruthlessness. She was no judge of men, of whom to trust and whom to use, but for the first few years of her reign she played a brilliant political game, either on her own, or with the advice and help of Maitland of Lethington, and her half-brother Lord James."

Queen Elizabeth refused to grant Mary's safe passage to Scotland unless she agreed to sign the previous year's Treaty of Edinburgh, which removed the French from Scotland and accepted that Elizabeth was the rightful monarch of England. This Mary refused. Another request from Mary for safe passage was granted by Elizabeth, but Mary had already left France without waiting for a reply. She had sent for the hereditary Great Admiral of Scotland, James Hepburn, Earl of Bothwell, to command the fleet that was to take her home to Scotland.

When Mary was boarding ship at Calais, a fishing boat sank in the harbour and those on board drowned. This was regarded as a bad omen. Before setting sail, she ordered that the lash should not be used on the galley slaves, whose condition she pitied. This unfamiliar kindness did not hinder progress, the voyage taking five days instead of the expected ten.

As the Scots fleet pulled away from France, there were more tearful scenes from Mary. Until the coast was finally out of sight she clung to the rail crying: "Adieu France! Adieu France! Je pense ne vous revoir jamais plus." (...I think I shall never see you again.)

Chapter Five

Sorrow, dolour, darkness

*T*he Scottish nobles and gentry had been advised to expect their Queen in the last days of August, when a suitable welcome should be ready. But the swiftness of the voyage caught everyone unawares. The approach of the Queen's vessels to Leith on the morning of August 19, 1561, was hidden from those on land by a thick mist.

It was a damp, miserable Tuesday, boding ill for the return of Scotland's monarch. To make matters worse, the Queen's favourite palfrey had been on a ship seized by the English off the Tyne, so that only an inferior old nag was available for her ride to Holyrood from Leith. But before even that horse could be made ready, Mary and her entourage had to spend some time at Leith while panic-struck subjects rushed around making arrangements, having been startled by the unexpected sound of cannon from her galleys announcing the arrival through the mist.

Andrew Lamb, a Leith merchant, came to the rescue of his Queen on her landing at The Shore, beside the King's Wark. He provided food and shelter for her and her entourage including the Four Maries, in his house at Water's Close. There is a magnificent centuries-old building on the site today, restored as the Lamb's House centre for old people, but it is probably a more recent building than the one where Mary Stuart dined. Leith, where Mary of Guise had lived, presented a sorry sight. The ravages of 1544 and the

44

Rough Wooing had still not been fully repaired, and much damage was still evident from the siege of 1559-60 when Leith had been defended by the French and Catholics against attack by the Protestants, supported by English forces. The Treaty of Edinburgh had ended the fighting.

Illustration 2 — Mary arriving in Scotland at the Port of Leith.

That night at Holyrood the Scots set out to try and make amends for the ill-prepared welcome of the morning. A band came with three-stringed fiddles to cheer up their Queen. As John Knox put it, a "company of most honest men, with instruments of music, and with musicians gave their salutations at her chamber windows, and that the Queen said that the melody liked her well, and she wished the same to be continued some nights after." (In the idiom of the time "liked" meant "pleased".)

Brantôme, one of the French party who accompanied Mary, put a different construction on these honest men and their music: "And worst of all, that at night when she wished to sleep, being lodged in the Abbey, there came under her window five or six hundred rogues from the town giving her a serenade of evil violins .... and began to sing psalms very badly."

The arrival of the tall — she stood just short of six feet — attractive Queen excited much admiration. Edinburgh was decorated with garlands and banners and a pageant was laid on for her delectation. At this stage there can be no doubt she was truly made welcome, but as early as her first Sunday in Scotland there was an unwelcome signal of future conflict. She had been careful, and perhaps had no option, to choose Protestants as her closest advisers in Scotland, and they accepted her wish to have Mass said privately for her. However Protestant ministers, especially Knox, were against this and when it was known that a Catholic service was to go ahead for the Queen at Holyrood on August 24 an angry mob gathered and had to be kept out, Mary's Protestant half-brother Lord James barring the way.

Mary declared next day that there should be no other interference with the form of public worship prevailing in the land following the Reformation, but in thus accepting that her country was Protestant she wanted her right accepted to enjoying private Catholic services for herself and her French visitors. Knox fulminated against Mary's religion from the pulpit of St Giles the following Sunday, resulting in a summons to an audience with the Queen.

In later describing Mary's arrival at Leith, Knox wrote: "The very face of heaven did manifestlie speak what comfort was brought to this country with hir — to wit, sorrow, dolour, darkness, and all impiety; for in the memory of man never was seyn a more dolorous

46

face of the heavens than was at her arryvall .... the myst was so thick that skairse mycht onie man espy another; and the sun was not seyn to shyne two days befoir nor two days after!"

Of course Knox, as the leading Protestant preacher whose mentor George Wishart had been done to death at Catholic hands, was hardly likely to approve the arrival of a Catholic monarch so soon after the hard-won Reformation. It must have seemed worse in his eyes that she was a woman, following his publication in Geneva in 1558 of *"The first blast of the trumpet against the monstrous regiment of women."* When living in England he had some deft explaining to do to cool the annoyance of Queen Elizabeth; it should be remembered that his view of women rulers had been coloured by "Bloody Mary" Tudor, under whom 300 Protestants had gone to the English stake in four years.

Knox, incidentally, seems to have had no objection to the company of women. Both his wives were teenagers when he married them. After the death of wife number one he married a girl more than 30 years his junior.

In the *"First Blast"* he wrote: "To promote a woman to beare rule, superioritie, dominion or empire above any realme, nation, or citie, is repugnant to nature, contumelie to God, a thing most contrarious to His reveled will and approved ordinance, and finallie it is the subversion of good order, of all equitie and justice."

A schoolmaster at Linlithgow, one Ninian Winzet, had to flee to the Continent, later becoming a Benedictine abbot, after publishing a riposte to Knox under perhaps the most unwieldy title ever: *"Last Blast of the Trumpet of God's Word against the usurped authorities of John Knox and his Calvinistic brethren intruding preachers etc put forth to the Congregation of the Protestants in Scotland by Ninian Winzet a Catholic priest born in Renfrew."* His popularity was not helped by another tract, which at least had the virtue of a snappier title: *"Is John Knox a lawful Minister?"*

47

Knox and the Queen of Scots had a long argument at Holyrood. He indicated that he was prepared
to accept a woman on the throne, provided the country was not brought to disaster. He was as well content
to live under her as Paul had been to live under Nero,
but subjects still had a right to oppose an unworthy

Illustration 3 — Mary and John Knox at Holyrood.

ruler. At one point she was in tears, but seems to have
found the debate stimulating. Knox answered with a
parable when Mary asked him if subjects should resist
their princes. He asked if children did harm by taking
away their father's sword when he went into a frenzy
and might have killed them. Mary responded: "I

perceive that my subjects shall obey you and not me and will do what they list and not what I command, and so must I be subject to them and not they to me."

One confrontation between Knox and the Queen followed his denunciation of dancing. Later Mary summoned Knox to explain a sermon in which he had attacked the possibility that she might marry a Catholic. Mary complained of his ingratitude to her, who had courted his favour, but Knox with "iron eyes beheld her weep in vain."

He said he was not master of himself in the pulpit, but must obey the commands of God who bade him speak plain and flatter no flesh. Knox declared that his vocation was to preach, not wait in the courts of princes or the chambers of ladies. The Queen said she granted him that, but what was he within the commonwealth of Scotland?

"A subject born within the same", came the reply, "and albeit, madam, neither baron, lord nor belted earl, yet hath God made me, however abject so ever in your eyes, a useful and profitable member. As such it is my duty to forewarn the people of danger: and, therefore, what I have said in public I repeat to your own face!

"Whenever the nobility of this realm so far forget themselves that you shall be subject to an unlawful husband, they do as much as in them lieth to renounce Christ, to banish the truth, betray the freedom of the realm, and perchance be but cold friends to yourself!"

On his way out Knox paused to address the grandly dressed ladies of the household: "Ah fair ladies, how pleasant were this life of yours if it should ever abide, and then in the end we might pass to heaven with all this gear! But fie on the knave Death! — that will come whether ye will or not: and when he hath laid on the arrest, then foul worms will be busy with this flesh, be it ever so fair and tender, and the silly soul, I fear, shall be feeble, that it can neither carry with it gold, garnishing, targating, pearl nor precious stone."

On another occasion Knox went on trial before Mary on a charge of treason. But the Privy Council found him not guilty. Not all meetings of Knox and the Queen involved conflict. In April 1563 they had a friendly discussion at Lochleven Castle.

Knox may have been offended by the frivolity and dancing of Mary's court, but she succeeded in charming pretty well everyone else. It was not just her beauty (the most beautiful princess in all Europe, the Venetian ambassador declared) and her joyous love of fun that won people over to her. Foreign observers in reports home praised her for her astute, wise rule. She went out of her way to placate her Protestant people, to the extent that Roman Catholic leaders overseas became impatient for her to try and restore their religion. She made no such move, but constantly stressed that in her personal life she remained a true Catholic.

During her first weeks in Scotland she went on a tour, first to her birthplace at Linlithgow Palace, then on to Stirling, Perth, Dundee, St Andrews and Falkland. She was given a warm welcome by many but the journey was marred by anti-Catholic demonstrations.

Her determination to show her acceptance of the fact of the Reformation was indicated by her choice of her closest advisers, both leading Protestants, Lord James, her brother, and William Maitland of Lethington, the political leader of the Reformation who became her Secretary of State. The latter, who was to marry Mary Fleming in 1567, was known as Michael Wily, a pun on Machiavelli, and an indication of how he was regarded.

Another indication of her support of public Protestantism in spite of her private Catholicism came on August 11, 1562, when she did something modern royalty does at this time of year. She went to the North. But this was no "Glorious Twelfth" hunting for grouse, for the expedition turned instead into a hunt for Scotland's leading Catholic lord with the object of defeating him. Hardly the action of a monarch set upon restoring Catholicism!

The Earl of Huntly, head of the Gordons,

dominated the North-east of Scotland. His son Sir John Gordon, who fancied himself as a possible husband for the Queen, escaped from prison where he had been incarcerated after a street brawl. Pursuing him gave an opportunity to move against the Gordons. Huntly and the Queen did not see eye-to-eye, in spite of being co-religionists, because the Gordons were an unruly lot, and Huntly was displeased by his cousin Mary's coolness towards his suggestions of re-introducing the Mass publicly. To move against him would seem a daring step, for besides his stewardship of the royal castles at Inverness and Inverlochy, he had several castles of his own including the "Gay Gordons" headquarters, Strathbogie Castle, near Huntly. Since 1549 he had held the earldom of Moray, but Mary had secretly awarded it to her brother Lord James early in 1562. The expedition to the North was a means of acquiring the lands of Moray for the new earl, whose position had not been advised to Huntly.

As Mary and Lord James headed by Stirling, Coupar Angus and Glamis towards Aberdeen ostensibly in pursuit of Sir John there was still a chance for Huntly to declare himself for the Queen, but instead he prepared a plot to kidnap her and have her forcibly married to his son. Sir John, meanwhile, surrendered, but then escaped and gathered a strong force of horsemen with the intention of abducting the Queen. Huntly and Sir John hoped that the Queen could be induced to rest at Strathbogie, where the Gordon coup could be put into effect. She was not so stupid as to fall for that one, and stopped off at Darnaway Castle instead, choosing this moment to make public that Lord James was Earl of Moray.

When Mary reached Inverness on September 11 she found access to her own castle barred by another of Huntly's sons, Alexander Gordon. This was treason, and Huntly was alarmed to hear of it because other chiefs were rallying to their Queen. She was admitted on the orders of a temporarily nervous Huntly.

Mary enjoyed her visit to Inverness, being much impressed by the clan chiefs and their Highlanders

51

who came to greet their Queen. The menace of Sir John Gordon and his nearby forces added spice to the sense of adventure. Here she cheerfully told the English ambassador Thomas Randolph, who did not enjoy the journey to these wild parts, that she regretted that she was not a man "to know what like it was to

Illustration 4 — Mary with her army in the Highlands.

lie all night in the fields, or to walk upon the causeway with a jack and knapschall (helmet), a Glasgow buckler and a broadsword."

She enjoyed her Highland journey so much that she was to return to Inverness in 1564, on the way to Beauly and Dingwall. On the 1562 trip, however, there was still the serious business of the Gordons to be tackled. She proceeded to the bishop's palace at Spynie, near Elgin, and returned to Aberdeen where there was no doubt about the warmth of the welcome. (On her previous arrival at Aberdeen she visited the university and was impressed enough to later bequeath Greek and Latin books to its library.)

Mary and the Earl of Moray sent for more forces including cannon to deal with Huntly, calling upon him in the meantime to surrender his own cannon at Strathbogie. Huntly spent his days at Strathbogie, but each night sheltered under a different roof, lest he be taken unawares. Some of Mary's men tried to surprise Huntly during his daytime meal at Strathbogie, but while they were noisily approaching the front door he was scrambling over a wall at the back of the castle where there was a horse ready for such an eventuality. He had no time to finish his meal, or put on his boots. An incredibly fat man, he must have presented some spectacle as he made his undignified, bootless departure over the castle wall.

Huntly and Sir John were outlawed, and the surrender of Strathbogie Castle was demanded. The Queen was sent the keys of Auchindoun and Findlater castles, but Huntly took to the hills and continued to defy his monarch. This part of the world was not so far from where Shakespeare imagined the witches making forecasts to Macbeth, and there were still witches about. Lady Huntly was given a prophecy by witches and acting upon it she urged her husband to attack the Queen's forces. However, the words of soothsayers and oracles should be treated with caution. Lady Huntly's witches said her husband would lie in the Tolbooth at Aberdeen with not a wound upon him, which the dear wife took to mean that he would be victorious in battle and would then ride safely into Aberdeen where he could rest the night unharmed. Unfortunately, the prophesy was true but not quite in the way that had been assumed. Just at the point when it became clear that the Gordons had lost the battle, the overweight Huntly took a heart attack and fell dead from his horse. So it was a lifeless, if wound-free, body that lay in the Aberdeen Tolbooth that night.

Sir John was executed for his part in the insurrection. Mary was required to attend, because of the nature of his offence, but she was sickened by the scene, collapsing in tears and having to be carried out. As treason against the crown required the presence of the accused, whether alive or dead, the body of Huntly — preserved in whisky, vinegar and spices — was taken to Edinburgh and stood trial! He was declared guilty and his belongings forfeited. More than three years after the battle of Corrichie, Huntly was finally buried at Elgin Cathedral.

Another execution followed a declaration of love for Mary in circumstances which suggested there was a Huguenot plot to blacken her reputation. Pierre de Châtelard, a poet who had praised her beauty in typically lavish terms, came back from France to visit her a second time. There seemed no harm in him on the previous occasion, but this time it was different. He arrived at Aberdeen with a book of his poems, and Mary gave him a gift as she often did to those about her. This was all very innocent, but then a routine check before the Queen went to her bedchamber revealed Châtelard hiding under the bed.

She banished him from her court, but that did not stop him following her to Burntisland where he burst in upon her and behaved so outrageously that she screamed hysterically for help. Later, he attempted to excuse his behaviour by saying that at Burntisland he only wanted to explain to the Queen that at Aberdeen he had felt tired and under her bed just happened to be a convenient place to rest. This feeble nonsense cut no ice at his trial and he was sentenced to death. Before being beheaded at St Andrews Châtelard quoted Ronsard's *"Hymn to Death"*, and then called out a farewell to "the most beautiful and the most cruel princess of the world." His last words were: "O cruelle Dame!"

Mary was depressed enough by the death of the Protestant poet, without the news a few days later that a Huguenot assassin had fulfilled an astrologer's prediction by shooting dead her uncle, Duke Francis de Guise.

Various illnesses did not help her mood in those sad days, but there were enjoyable times, too, including the thrill of the chase when she went hunting at Falkland and Blair Atholl. There were masques and entertainments at Holyrood and elsewhere to allow her to display her sense of fun. One great entertainment came in 1564 when she held an open-air banquet at the foot of Arthur's Seat for the nuptials of John, fifth Lord Fleming, Lord High Chamberlain, and Elizabeth, only daughter and heiress of Robert, Master of Ross.

There are tales, too, of her going out disguised as a man to wander the streets to observe what went on without the formal arrangements of a royal procession. Such stories are told of many monarchs in many lands.

So, in spite of the bouts of sadness, Mary might have continued to lead a reasonably good life. She had become truly popular. Her care to support the continuation of the Protestant religion as the public form of worship in the land, her judicious handling of issues which came before her, and her careful diplomacy through which she attempted to persuade Elizabeth to name Mary as heir to the English throne, all helped create the impression of a successful monarch. Even John Knox recorded his admiration for the bravery with which she led her troops against Huntly.

But it was all to go so disastrously wrong. The move to real tragedy came with the inevitable second marriage. An heir to the throne was essential, but who was to be father to the bairn? There were real fears that she might marry a Catholic, a strong possibility if the groom came from overseas. A Spanish match was mentioned. So was Charles, Archduke of Austria. There was talk of a French king for Scotland. Even Queen Elizabeth's favourite, Robert Dudley, who was created Earl of Leicester, was in the running. The ambitious Countess of Lennox was keen to see her son make a royal marriage. He was Mary's cousin, and with Tudor and Stuart ancestry was also in line for the throne of England — Henry Stuart, Lord Darnley.

55

Whoever Mary married it would displease someone, but it might be said that her choice was a fatal one for it led directly to the misfortunes that were to follow. In marrying Darnley, on July 29, 1565, Mary displeased Elizabeth, who was alarmed that Darnley's own claim to the English throne strengthened that of Mary. And yet it had been thought in some quarters that Elizabeth had really wanted this match between Mary and the "long lad" who like Mary was a grandchild of Margaret Tudor (Mary's grandfather was James IV and Darnley's was Archibald, Earl of Angus, Margaret Tudor's second husband). The marriage was another of those occasions when Mary sent off a letter, then acted without waiting for a reply. She had written to the Pope for approval for the marriage, due to her groom being a relative, but went ahead before hearing of a papal blessing.

Darnley's Catholicism was also a cause of anger among the Protestant lords. Now the recently created Earl of Moray switched from being his sister's close adviser to being her enemy. Moray and other Protestant leaders rebelled against their Queen and the newly created King Henry. Mary's army set out from Edinburgh on August 26, 1565. What followed came to be known as the "Chase-about Raids" because the royal forces chased the rebels around for a few weeks, before Moray fled to England on October 6. Elizabeth granted him sanctuary, but gave him a ticking off for rebelling against his Queen!

Another name associated so sadly with Mary's fate returned to the scene at the time of the "Chase-about" rebellion. Bothwell, who had arranged her voyage to Scotland, was allowed back into favour, having been banished from court after his part in a fight concerning the Earl of Arran's mistress. Bothwell was the cause of a row between Mary and Darnley, who favoured his father as a military leader over Bothwell who had been backed by the Queen. (Darnley's father, the Earl of Lennox, was undistinguished militarily and had been exiled to England after backing Henry VIII during the "Rough Wooing".)

56

At first the marriage appeared happy enough, and the Queen was soon pregnant. Then it became clear that the decision to marry Darnley was more than a political mistake — it was a personal disaster for Mary. It is recorded that he was disgustingly rude to her during a dinner at Traquair House, comparing the mother-to-be of his child to a cow expecting a calf. The arrogant Darnley became contemptuous of his wife, and took to associating with prostitutes.

Now it happened that Mary had employed an Italian, David Riccio, since 1561. A musician, he had become a secretary to the Queen. He was also one of a band of musicians and singers who helped brighten her life at Holyrood, and Darnley grew to be jealous. His increasingly hostile opinion of Riccio coincided with a growing fear among some Protestant lords that the Italian was in touch with Philip of Spain and would encourage the return of Catholicism to Scotland.

On the night of March 9, 1566, the heavily pregnant Queen was relaxing on a couch during a supper party at Holyrood with a number of friends including Riccio when Darnley burst in. With him was Patrick, Lord Ruthven, who was ill and near death. "Let it please Your Majesty that yon David come forth from your privy chamber where he hath been overlong", said Ruthven, who wore armour beneath his cloak. Mary demanded of her husband what this invasion of her chambers was all about, but it was Ruthven who replied, claiming that the Queen was dishonoured by her association with Riccio. Ruthven shouted: "Lay not your hands on me for I will not be handled." This was addressed to one of Mary's party who tried to stop Ruthven approaching the by now terrified Riccio. Ruthven drew his dagger and the other conspirators charged in.

The secretary tried to cling to the Queen's skirts, screaming for her to protect him, but he was dragged away. Darnley restrained his wife, while another of the conspirators plucked Darnley's knife from his belt and plunged it into Riccio. They dragged the squealing, wounded Riccio into the next room, plunging daggers into him more than 50 times. His lifeless form was allowed to slump to the floor, and the Queen was ordered to stop shrieking for help or she would be "cut into collops" (small pieces of meat in a stew). "His death shall cost you dear", she called out.

Later she was to say: "Farewell tears. We must now think on revenge." Bothwell, who had nothing to do with the plot, was heard to declare angrily that night that what was done was done in Darnley's name. These comments might be significant in view of what was to happen the following year. And the help now given to Mary by Bothwell in her hour of need caused her to be strongly favourable towards him.

Word came to her at Holyrood that Bothwell was ready with a strong force of supporters. She persuaded the nervous Darnley, who began to worry about his involvement in Riccio's murder, that it was in his best interests to help her escape. She alarmed her treacherous husband with the thought that the conspirators might kill him next. When they got away from Holyrood, he panicked and rode away ahead

In spite of the hazard to her pregnancy from the distress of the murder followed by the horse ride to Dunbar Castle, where Bothwell was ready to protect her, she seems to have regarded the escape as exciting and next morning found her cheerfully demanding eggs to fry up for the men. This escapade established her as a romantic heroine in her own lifetime, a reputation the intervening centuries have done nothing to diminish.

The attack on Riccio was really a plot against the Queen, who had been about to convene the Estates, the Scottish Parliament, to forfeit lands of those who had opposed her. It is also possible that at least some thought the stress of the event might cause a miscarriage which in those times might well have meant her death. But, her supremacy as Queen again acknowledged, she returned at the head of 8,000 men to Edinburgh where she gave birth on June 19, 1566, to a prince. James was born with a caul over his face, believed to be such a sign of good luck that even in recent times fishermen and other seamen were anxious to buy one as a charm. It was said that if someone owned, or had been born with, a caul they would never drown.

Childbirth was such a hazard in the sixteenth century that before the birth in Edinburgh Castle Mary

Illustration 5 — Mary and Darnley flee from Holyrood.

made a will, which included provision for Darnley, her half-brother Moray who had been forgiven for his recent temporary rebellion, her other Scottish and French relatives, and the four Maries, among others. The cradle Mary used for James is still to be seen at Traquair House in Peebles-shire.

Many nasty rumours surrounded the infant prince. James was later known in some quarters as having the wisdom of Solomon, "the son of David", implying that Riccio had been the father. In 1830 during building work at the castle a coffin containing a baby's remains was found in a wall, implying to some

Illustration 6 — Mary with baby son (destined to be James VI and I) at Edinburgh Castle — citizens lit bonfires to celebrate the birth.

that there might have been truth in the suggestion that Mary's baby died and was replaced by another. However, there is no reason to believe that James was other than Mary's son. When Darnley came to see the new-born prince she declared to him before witnesses: "My Lord, God has given you and me a son, begotten by none but you. I protest to God, and as I shall answer to Him at the great day of judgment, this is your son, and no other man's."

Sir James Melville was sent on Mary's behalf to take the news of the birth to Queen Elizabeth at Greenwich, where the Virgin Queen uttered her famous response: "The Queen of Scotland is lighter of a fair son and I am but a barren stock."

Elizabeth, although not present at the christening of James at Stirling Castle on December 17, 1566, was chosen as a godparent by Mary and sent a superb gold font as a gift. This later was melted down to pay Mary's soldiers! Darnley took no part in the baptism ceremony, although he was at Stirling at the time. It was a Catholic service, but Mary refused to allow the priest to spit in the baby's mouth as had been the custom.

In the period between the birth and the baptism Mary visited Jedburgh where she became seriously ill and was thought to be near death, before recovering.

As part of the propaganda war later waged against her it was said that she was having an affair at this time with James Hepburn, Earl of Bothwell, but this was quite untrue. While she was at Jedburgh for a sitting of the law courts in October, news was brought that Bothwell was wounded while attempting to bring to justice the "thievis and malefactouris of Liddesdale." Bothwell, who besides being Lord High Admiral of Scotland, was also Sheriff of Berwick, Haddington and Edinburgh, Bailie of Lauderdale, Lieutenant Warden of the Marches and Keeper of Hermitage Castle, had been forced to release his captives from Hermitage after he was injured. After some days' preparation, Mary rode to Hermitage to confer with Bothwell, in the company of Moray, other Privy Councillors and an armed escort. Owing to the danger posed by the proximity of feuding Border families, she returned to a house which still stands in Jedburgh the same day, the 50 miles round trip perhaps helping to bring on the illness which followed. Her enemies claimed she had ridden off to Hermitage at a moment's notice in order to snatch a passionate interlude with her lover, but like so much else that was later to be said against her this was a despicable lie.

Mary did, however, come to depend on Bothwell, and this was to prove unwise. Her relationship with Darnley had become severely strained, but on hearing

Illustration 7 — Mary rides to Hermitage Castle to see Bothwell.

that he was seriously ill in Glasgow, probably in the house known as Provand's Lordship, her heart seems to have softened and she went to nurse him. Presumably she was unaware that the disease from which he suffered was syphillis, for which the treatment was mercury, a poisonous liquid metal which was almost as bad as the venereal disease which it cured. The combination of "the French disease" or "la maladie Anglaise" with mercury poisoning would certainly make him very ill indeed.

Darnley's condition improved enough for him to be persuaded to come to Edinburgh to complete his convalescence. Mary had wanted him to go to Craigmillar Castle which would have been suitable for an invalid, but instead he went to Kirk o' Field, a house just within the Flodden Wall to the south side of Edinburgh. Mary visited him frequently, seeing him for the last time on the night of Sunday, February 9, 1567, the last before Lent and therefore a time of carnival. As Mary returned to Holyrood for the masque following the wedding of her favourite valet Bastian Pages and Christiana Hogg, she did not know that someone had been stocking up gunpowder in the house at Kirk o' Field. Darnley was due to go to Holyrood next day, but in the early hours of the morning there was a terrible explosion which woke the citizens of Edinburgh and the residents at the Palace of Holyroodhouse.

Those who rushed from their beds to the scene found that the building which housed the king had been blown up. Indeed, on November 5, 1605, on hearing the rumours of the Guy Fawkes plot, Mary's son, by then James VI of Scotland and I of England, is said to have remarked: "I remember that my father died by gunpowder. Search the basements!" But Darnley, who must have been disturbed by some commotion just before the explosion, and tried to escape, was found strangled outside the house at Kirk o' Field.

Bothwell was one of those guilty of the killing, but when he stood trial on April 12 he was acquitted. His chief accuser, Darnley's father, the Earl of Lennox, was not present, and Bothwell's many armed supporters were there to intimidate any who might have sought to confirm his guilt. Events now moved quickly to personal disaster for Mary.

On April 24, when she was on her way to Edinburgh after visiting her baby son at Stirling (the last time she was to see him, although she did not know it then), Bothwell and a large party of his men abducted her. He told her she had to be protected from danger in the capital, and she allowed him to escort her to the safety of Dunbar Castle. Once there, he raped her. It was part of his strategy to force her to marry him, to fulfil his ambition to be king.

Illustration 8 — Bothwell and his army abduct Mary.

He also told her that marriage to him would be supported by the leading figures in Scotland, unlike her wedding to Darnley. As proof Bothwell produced a document in support of his marriage plan signed by eight bishops, nine earls and seven barons. This paper came to be known as the Ainslie Bond — after

Ainslie's Tavern in Edinburgh where it seems Bothwell plied the signatories with food and drink before persuading them to append their names. To clear the way for the marriage, Bothwell's wife Jean Gordon agreed to divorce him on the grounds of his adultery with a maid in a kitchen at Crichton Castle.

It was all done in great haste, and when John Craig, a minister who was a colleague of John Knox, was told to publish the marriage banns he publicly accused Bothwell of rape, adultery and collusion with his wife. Craig was a brave man. Bothwell threatened to kill him.

Bothwell led Mary into Edinburgh in a way that suggested to observers that she was his prisoner. Some said he had used black magic to influence her. Certainly, as she went to their marriage at Holyrood on May 15, she appeared to be in some kind of trance. Bothwell's powerful personality had dominated her when she was suffering sickness and melancholy after the death of Darnley.

Sir James Melville, who had been forcibly detained in another part of Dunbar Castle while Bothwell assaulted the Queen, reported later that Mary felt she had to marry Bothwell "seeing he had ravished her and laid with her against her will." After the marriage the French ambassador Philip du Croc wrote about Mary's unhappiness to Catherine de Medicis: ".... being secluded all day with the Earl of Bothwell she cried out aloud for someone to give her a knife so she could kill herself."

On June 15, 1567, at Carberry Hill, near Musselburgh, troops backing the Queen and Bothwell faced the superior forces of other Scottish leaders who had decided to rise up against the marriage and overthrow Bothwell. Rather than allow battle to commence, Mary gave herself up and Bothwell escaped. Mary thought she would be allowed to continue as Queen, but on the way into Edinburgh it became apparent that she was to be robbed of her throne.

She was treated rudely by the soldiers and in Edinburgh there was a hostile crowd. Wearing a riding tunic and a short red petticoat, because there was no proper woman's clothing available at Dunbar Castle where she had been before being treacherously persuaded to come to Carberry, she was dragged into the Black Turnpike, a house in the Royal Mile. "I am your Queen, your own native princess; oh, suffer me not to

Illustration 9 — The pressure mounts on Mary after the death of Darnley.

be abused thus!" she cried, before she was locked in a room. That night she was seen at a window, her face pale from fear and her eyes swollen with tears. Those who witnessed her were moved to pity, and the mood of the fickle mob changed in her favour.

To appease the crowd she was taken to Holyrood, but it was only a temporary move because from there she was transferred on June 17 to the Douglas island stronghold, Lochleven Castle. On July 24, during her first distressing weeks of imprisonment, she was forced to abdicate in favour of her son. Lord Lindsay, who had plotted against Riccio, "crushed her tender arm with his steel glove and compelled her under terror of death to sign her abdication", according to one version.

Five days later her son, little more than a year old, was crowned James VI at Stirling, John Knox preaching the coronation sermon. Again Scotland was under the nominal rule of an infant monarch, while the real power in the land was the Regent, this time Moray who was now effectively the king he had always thought he ought to be. Mary had remained true to Bothwell, paying no heed to those who wanted her to divorce him. She was pregnant, and did not wish to lose the legitimacy of the child. However, at Loch Leven she gave birth to still-born twins, and became very ill.

She was to recover, aided by the discovery that she still had friends who would help her escape. If she could get free, and raise an army of support there was a chance to regain the throne. She could justifiably claim that the abdication was illegal because she had been forced to accept it under duress. One escape attempt failed, when a boatman became suspicious of the long, dainty, white hands of the tall Queen disguised as a "washer woman". Then on May 2, 1568, she got away, helped on the island by 16-year-old Willie Douglas, a foundling adopted by her jailer's family, and ashore by George Douglas, another of the family Willie succeeded in stealing the castle key from Mary's jailer Sir William Douglas, and safely got Mary across to the shore by boat. (Assorted keys since fished out of the loch are said to be the key Willie threw away, but there is no proof.)

The half-brother of Mary Seton, George, fifth Lord Seton, was also in the plan to rescue his Queen. After crossing the Forth at Queensferry she rested for the rest of the night at "Loyal Seton's" West Lothian castle of Niddry, near Winchburgh, before continuing to Hamilton. Now, with thousands of men rallying to her cause, she seemed sure of victory, but Moray's men were better organised and in spite of being out-

Illustration 10 — Willie rows Mary to freedom!

numbered they gained the high ground at Langside south of Glasgow and on May 13, 1568, defeated the Marian forces there.

She fled to the safety of Dumfriesshire, sleeping on the ground when she had to, with little to eat or drink. An old woman gave Mary milk on the way, and a grateful Queen arranged with Lord Herries that the woman should live rent free in her cottage for the rest of her days for this kindness.

It had long been Mary's wish to meet Elizabeth, to whom the Queen of Scots had frequently sent friendly letters addressed to England's "richt excellent, rycht heich and michtie Princesse, oure derrest sister and cousyn." Another letter was sent, seeking permission for Mary to come to England for safety. Then after resting at Dundrennan Abbey, Mary crossed the Solway Firth in a fishing boat to Workington, without waiting for a reply from Elizabeth. Mary was sure Elizabeth would meet her and give help.

But, sadly, there was to be no meeting; there was to be no help.

Chapter Six

A base executioner

Mary at first had no cause to think that her flight to England was to mean incarceration. She and her 16 faithful followers spent their first night after leaving Scotland on May 16, 1568, at Workington Hall, then rode on next day to Cockermouth Hall, where on May 18 she held court for the Duke of Norfolk's sister Lady Scroope and the ladies of the district who flocked to pay their respects to the Queen of Scots.

When she had reigned in Scotland her wardrobe included a huge variety of magnificent dresses, many of cloth of silver and cloth of gold, and she possessed an amazing range of jewels, including three sets of diamonds, one of rubies and diamonds, one of rubies and pierced pearls, one of rubies, diamonds and pearls, another of sapphires, ropes rather than strings of black pearls, filigree gold ornaments, diamond crosses, and a table of diamonds in a ring. Many of her treasures were pilfered by confederate lords after her forced abdication. (The finest jewel was the Great Harry diamond, given her by Henry II of France when she married the Dauphin. Mary had it mounted in the Scottish crown, but its ownership later became the subject of dispute. James VI and I had it fitted with some of Queen Elizabeth's jewellery into a piece known as the Mirror of Great Britain, which was pawned at the end of his reign when the royal finances were in ruins.)

Among clothes left behind in her flight from Scotland were 69 dresses, 15 skirts, 44 separate pairs of sleeves and 36 pairs of shoes. Henry Fletcher, the rich merchant who owned Cockermouth Hall, noted the bedraggled state of the clothing Mary had brought, and presented her with a new robe of crimson velvet, for which kindness Fletcher's son would be knighted by James when he ascended the throne of England.

Mary's progress from Cockermouth to Carlisle resembled a triumphant procession. It was only after she was securely in Carlisle Castle, where her presence is commemorated in the name of Queen Mary's Tower, that it became clear that the soldiers who provided the escort from Cockermouth were not just there to protect her. They were there to make sure she did not escape.

Mary, not yet 26, had begun the illegal imprisonment that was to last until two months after her 44th birthday. As a focus for potential Catholic rebellion, and a claimant to the English throne, she had become a hazardous liability to the English Queen.

Carlisle was deemed to be too close to the Scottish border for English comfort. Mary may have lost the Battle of Langside, but only because the confederate troops stole a march on the Marian men and held a strong position from which her progress could be cut off. Mary, however, had been supported by 6,000 men to Regent Moray's 4,000. There was always the possibility that a captive who could muster such backing within days of escape from Loch Leven might again escape and raise an army.

So she was moved south, sadly not to the audience she so craved with her English cousin. After being taken to Bolton Castle, a relatively comfortable fourteenth century pile which still stands over Wensleydale in North Yorkshire, she was transferred further south to the custody of the man who was to be her kindly jailer for most of the rest of her time in England, George Talbot, Earl of Shrewsbury.

71

Several of his residences where she was detained at various times were relatively pleasant: the grand Derbyshire houses of Chatsworth and Wingfield, and Sheffield Castle and Sheffield Manor, which were quite close to each other. One other she detested: the damp, ruinous Staffordshire castle at Tutbury, where the conditions destroyed her steadily declining health. Chatsworth, incidentally, was not the even grander building that stands there now, although Queen Mary's Bower in the grounds marks the site of her little garden.

At first the formidable second wife of Shrewsbury, Bess of Hardwick, was friendly with Mary. Beautiful embroidery which they sewed together is now on display at Hardwick Hall and Oxburgh Hall, Norfolk. Later they were to fall out, Bess making accusations that Shrewsbury and Mary were rather too friendly. Shrewsbury had said: "The Queen of Scots coming to my charge will make me soon grey-headed." He frequently complained of the expense of keeping her, and the substantial retinue of her court-in-exile, because the cost far exceeded the allowance provided. However, he let her make a number of visits to Buxton, where the spa waters might help tackle her dropsy, arthritis and rheumatic gout, and when she was in better health he allowed her to go riding and hawking, and enjoy archery.

On these trips out Mary gave gifts of alms, and even conducted her own annual Maundy ceremony. Reports of all this alarmed the English Court because it was feared that Mary's generosity might win support to her cause. It was during bouts of official nervousness that the order would come through for a transfer to the hated Tutbury (where there are still remains of the fourteenth century stronghold).

Events elsewhere over which Mary had no control but which involved her, characterised her period of detention. In October 1568 she was tried at York in her absence on a trumped up charge of murdering Darnley. Her Scottish enemies, anxious not only to frame Mary but to turn attention away from their own real guilt in the Kirk o' Field plot, produced "evidence" in the shape of letters supposedly written by Mary to Bothwell plotting Darnley's death. Or rather they produced copies of letters. The originals very conveniently disappeared. Known as "The Casket Letters" because it was claimed they were found in a silver casket belonging to Mary these consisted mainly of the writings of a mistress Bothwell had spurned, carefully edited and revamped to give the impression Mary had written them. The forger's task took some time, explaining the interval of several months between the discovery of the casket and the revelation of what it supposedly contained.

There were plots in Mary's favour, too, but they did her no good. The last of them led to her death. The Duke of Norfolk planned to marry Mary, whom he never met, provided she divorced Bothwell first. Mary was sent to Tutbury when Elizabeth found out, and Norfolk went to the Tower of London (where Elizabeth had been imprisoned in 1554, coming to the throne four years later after narrowly escaping execution). The duke was later released, but broke his agreement to have nothing more to do with notions of freeing Mary by joining a plot for Mary arranged by Roberto Ridolfi, a London-based Florentine banker. Norfolk was executed in 1572.

In 1585 Mary was back at Tutbury, with the Puritan Sir Amyas Paulet as her unsympathetic jailer in place of Shrewsbury. Then Elizabeth's spymaster Sir Francis Walsingham, who could have taught today's CIA and KGB a lot, set a trap. Walsingham got a Burton-on-Trent brewer to pretend to be her friend, by smuggling letters in and out inside ale barrels. Mary was then tricked into accepting a plot by Sir Anthony Babington, a Catholic squire who had been her page at Sheffield, to free her with the support of Philip II of Spain. All the while Secretary of State Walsingham was intercepting the letters, having them copied, and pulling the strings by which he successfully paved the way for Mary's path to the executioner's block. She was taken to Tixall, then on September 25,

1586, was transferred to her last castle, Fotheringhay in Northamptonshire.

There was never any real danger to Elizabeth, because the whole intricate web of deceit was under the control of Walsingham, but the unfortunate Babington was executed and Mary went on trial at Fother-

Illustration 11 — Mary forwards a spirited defence at her trial.

inghay in what was a travesty of justice. She said her only crime was to have earnestly wished for liberty, a plea which meant nothing to the hardened hearts of England's Parliament. Both Houses urged Elizabeth to sign a death warrant for Mary, but she had no wish to do this, being fearful of the consequences of killing a sister Queen. The death warrant was slipped in among routine papers for her signature, which allowed Elizabeth to put on a Pontius Pilate act later, washing her hands of Mary's death.

The wording of the warrant made it clear that it was at the urging of Parliament, not the English Queen, that Mary was to be executed. However, Elizabeth's attempts to distance herself from the fatal decision both before and after hold no water for the cynical. She had suggested to Paulet that he should shorten Mary's life, which would have relieved Elizabeth of responsibility, but the Puritan had declared he could never "make so foul a shipwreck of my conscience to shed blood without law or warrant."

Other developments over which she had no control were to tell against Mary, including a papal decision to excommunicate Elizabeth and relieve English Catholics of any obligation to her. In 1572 the St Bartholomew's Day massacre of French Protestants caused new opposition to Mary, and led to Elizabeth's decision to lend Scotland heavy cannons to besiege Edinburgh Castle which had been held for Mary. The cannon fire caused such damage that the castle had to be surrendered in May, 1573.

By a supreme irony, it had been kept for the Marians by William Maitland of Lethington, who was instrumental in overthrowing Mary at Carberry and is widely believed to be the architect of the Casket Letters frame-up, and Sir William Kirkcaldy of Grange, the brilliant military leader who successfully commanded the confederates against Mary at Langside, but later had a change of heart with Maitland and decided to back her to the death. The military man, Kirkcaldy, was executed. The politician, Maitland, avoided execution by dying, "in the old Roman way" by poison at his own hand, some said.

And what of others involved with Mary over the dramatic years? Mary Seton — "the finest dresser of a woman's head of hair that is to be seen in any country" — spent most of Mary's detention with her, the only Marie to go to England. Mary Seton was finally persuaded to go to France, where she died years later an old, impoverished spinster. John Knox died in 1572. Moray was assassinated at Linlithgow in 1570. Bothwell, failing to raise support in Scotland's Scandinavian islands in Orkney and Shetland, also tried without success to get backing in Denmark, Norway and Sweden. The relatives of his one-time mistress Anna Thronsden caught up with him for his spurning of her years before and he spent his last years chained up in a Danish dungeon in a position which prevented him from standing up or lying down. He died insane, and now his partly-decomposed remains stare out through a glass-lidded coffin in a Danish crypt from the sixteenth century to this. Philip II of Spain mounted the Spanish Armada in 1588 in vengeance for Mary's death. James Douglas, Earl of Morton, one of those guilty of Riccio's murder, became Regent in Scotland in 1572, but was executed in 1581 for the killing of Darnley.

Mary's son James was sent many presents by her when she was captive in England, but he was never allowed to receive any of them. George Buchanan, a scholar who had praised Mary's beauty when he was part of her court, was James's tutor and sought to turn him against his mother by feeding the boy wicked lies, which Buchanan also wrote against Mary for general consumption. Some of his nonsense still sticks to Mary's reputation, without a shred of justification.

James was later to reject Buchanan's poison for what it was, and after succeeding Elizabeth on the English throne in 1603 he rehabilitated his mother's unjustly slighted place in history. He had the huge lead coffin with her remains transferred from Peterborough Cathedral to Westminster Abbey in London, where the big stone memorial he arranged gives her a proper position among other monarchs.

After writing her last letter, to her brother-in-law Henry III of France, in which she insisted that her Catholic faith and her right to the English crown were the two reasons for her being condemned, Mary was led to her death, on the morning of February 8, 1587.

She felt she was dying for her faith, and had become composed for this fate during weeks when Elizabeth had shed tears at the possibility of Mary's execution! Afterwards Elizabeth was to imprison the clerk who presented the death warrant for signature, and threw herself into genuine grief when there was rejoicing in the streets of London at Mary's demise. (When an emissary from Elizabeth went to Scotland to explain that the killing of the Queen of Scots had been done without the knowledge of the English Queen, James refused to give the man an audience.)

On that dreadful Wednesday in Fotheringhay Castle, which was later demolished to leave only token evidence of the site of the awful deed, Mary went quietly with a black satin dress and white veil, carrying a crucifix and a prayer book, to the place of execution. She pardoned the executioner and with the help of her lady-of-the-bedchamber, Jane Kennedy, who blindfolded her eyes, Mary knelt and placed her head on the block in front of the assembled witnesses. She had undressed to a red petticoat. "In manus tuas, Domine, confide spiritum meum", Mary said.

The first blow of the axe nicked the back of her head. "Sweet Jesus" were the last words she uttered. The second stroke almost severed her neck. The executioner's third movement of the axe was to hack it back and forth until the last sinews parted her head from her body. He grabbed the head by its auburn wig, and the head with its short grey hair fell to the floor, where it lay with the lips moving silently for some minutes. "So perish all the Queen's enemies", shouted the Dean of Peterborough, supposedly a man of God. A pet Skye terrier suddenly wriggled out from under the petticoat of its mistress, who had loved animals, and lay down between the head and the body. The dog refused to move willingly and pined away to death, declining food.

On March 12 at a Requiem Mass in the black-draped Cathedral of Notre Dame in Paris the Archbishop of Bourges, Renaud de Beaune; recalled the happy marriage there of 29 years before and spoke of

Mary's piteous death — "the axe of a base executioner mangling the form of her who was doubly a Queen."

Illustration 12 — Mary at her execution — John Mackays impression of this tragic day.

Chapter Seven

Princely Mansions and Old Towers

*T*he story of Mary Queen of Scots — "undoubtedly one of the most romantic figures of British history" according to the American *"Newsweek"* magazine — has inspired writers, poets and artists for more than 400 years, and will no doubt continue to do so. New light may yet be shed, there being a wealth of material available in addition to the substantial amount of information held in Edinburgh by the Scottish Record Office and the National Library of Scotland.

There can still be surprises. For example, in 1981 a previously unrecorded specimen of a rare Scottish coin, a silver testoon minted in 1553 with a likeness of Mary on it, turned up in Switzerland. Exhibitions and other events in many places associated with Mary during 1987, quatercentenary of her death, will undoubtedly have sparked off interest, possibly leading to new developments.

So there is much to find out about Mary. Those who want to know more will discover many books, notably the highly readable definitive history by Lady Antonia Fraser *"Mary Queen of Scots"* (Weidenfeld & Nicholson, also in Methuen paperback). Other titles in clude *"Mary Queen of Scots"* by Alan Bold (Wayland Publishers), *"Mary Queen of Scots, the Fair Devil of Scotland"* by Jean Plaidy (Robert Hale & Co), *"The Needlework of Mary Queen of Scots"* by Margaret Swain (Van Nostrand Reinhold) and *"Queen of Scots"* by Rosalind K Marshall (Her Majesty's Stationery Office). In *"The Casket Letters"* (Vision Press) M.H.Armstrong Davison examines the Kirk o' Field story in detail and concludes that Mary was innocent of Darnley's murder. HMSO and the Historic Buildings and Monuments section of the Scottish Development Department publish guides to buildings of interest, and there are other guides published by a variety of organisations and individuals.

But what makes discovery about Mary Stuart so exciting is that buildings which were known to her can be visited. It is possible to step through the very doorways by which she entered, and walk within the walls which gave her shelter in happy times and sad.

Writing more than 120 years ago a Scottish clergyman, the Rev John Marius Wilson, described the many historic properties which dot the map of Scotland as including "magnificent, princely mansions" and "old towers". Here is a selection of some of those associated with the incredible tale of the Queen of Scots:-

Alloa Tower: In Alloa House grounds. At least 500 years old. Fire in 1800 destroyed later parts and a portrait of Mary, who knew Alloa.

Arbroath Abbey: Founded in 1176 by William the Lion, and dedicated to St Thomas of Canterbury, the abbey was the setting for the signing of the historic Declaration of Arbroath in 1320 when the Scottish barons vowed to maintain the independence of Scotland. Mary visited in 1562 on the way from Aberdeen to Edinburgh.

Balquhain Castle: Now ruined keep where Mary spent night before Battle of Corrichie.

Balvenie Castle: Amid malt whisky country at Duff-town, visited by Mary for two nights in 1562. Mostly fifteenth and sixteenth century, but previous castle of Mortlach already on site by 1304.

Beauly Priory, Invernesshire: Founded in 1230. Latin title: Monasterium de Bello Loco (Monastery of the beautiful place). On being told this on a visit in 1564 Mary admired the beautiful setting and remarked: "Oui, c'est un beau lieu."

Blair Castle: Dates from 1269, but present appearance is Victorian. Associations with Bonnie Prince Charlie and Queen Victoria as well as Mary. Seat of Duke of Atholl, who has Britain's only private "army".

Borthwick Castle near Gorebridge, Midlothian: Restored as a private residence in the nineteenth century, Borthwick is the tallest tower house in Scotland and an impressive castle. Dates from fifteenth century, and includes an enormous hall with a huge hooded fireplace. Mary and Bothwell came here after marriage. On a later occasion Bothwell escaped from here when pursued by confederate forces. Mary was left behind and fled to join him two days later, disguised as a man. Off A7 road at Middleton.

Rossend Castle, Burntisland, Fife: Complete with Queen Mary's Room where Châtelard surprised her, would have been demolished by the former Burntisland Town Council but for a public inquiry in 1971. Restored by Ian Begg as his architectural firm's offices.

Cakemuir Castle near Dalkeith, Midlothian: Mary supposedly rested in this sixteenth century tower four miles South-east of Pathhead after flight from Borthwick in 1567.

Carberry Hill near Musselburgh: A memorial stone marks Mary's surrender.

Castle Campbell: Renamed by fifteenth century Act of Scottish Parliament, this Ancient Monument north of Dollar beside land now administered by National

Trust for Scotland, was previously Castle Gloom, and stands by waters of Burn of Care and Burn of Sorrow. Knox preached here in 1556.

Cessnock Castle, near Galston, Ayrshire: Mary visited here after Langside.

Cleish Castle, four miles South-west of Kinross: Mary came by after escape from Lochleven Castle.

Craignethan Castle: Mary may have been here the night before Langside. Beside Nethan Water about four miles from Lanark, this Ancient Monument is better known as Tillietudlem, the name given by Sir Walter Scott in *"Old Mortality"*.

Crichton Castle, Midlothian: The dramatic setting high above the River Tyne helps make this one-time stronghold of Bothwell's an awe-inspiring sight. Students of architecture will find it instructive to note the way the fifteenth century tower was added to in later centuries in a different style from Craigmillar Castle. The oldest section includes Scotland's worst dungeon, a small space high in the midst of an icy cold wall where unfortunates werre pushed into total darkness through a tiny door. Known as Massie More, it had a slit to admit air and the smell of cooking from the kitchen above. Mary attended a wedding at Crichton in 1562, and may have been here on honeymoon with Darnley. The famous internal courtyard wall of diamond-shaped stones came later, copied from the Palazzo dei Diamanti at Ferrara in Italy, also built in the 1580s. This important castle is near an historic collegiate church two miles South-west of Pathhead. Crichton Castle is praised by Scott in *"Marmion"*.

Crookston Castle: South-east of Paisley and well out of sight of Langside, but in *"The Abbot"* Scott had Mary watching the battle from here. She viewed the contest from Cathcart. Mary may have visited Crookston with Darnley.

Darnaway Castle: Mary held court in 1562 at this seat of the Earls of Moray in the Findhorn Valley near Forres.

Doune Castle: Fourteenth and fifteenth century Perthshire fortress visited by Mary.

Drumlanrig Castle: The Dumfriesshire home of the Dukes of Buccleuch and Queensberry acquired its present form between 1679 and 1691, although there are traces of the structure visited by Mary during her tour of the largely Catholic South-west in 1563.

Drummond Castle: South of Crieff. Visited by Mary.

Dumbarton Castle: Dumbarton Rock is a volcanic plug, like those at Edinburgh and Stirling which have also supported fortifications for centuries. But Dumbarton has a longer recorded history as a fortress than anywhere else in the British Isles. The military quit in 1865 but came back in the two world wars. Most of what stands here now is of seventeenth and eighteenth century date, but fragments of pottery more than 1,500 years old have been found and there are two gravestones which are at least 900 years old. Known once as Alcluith (Rock of Clyde) it was also Dun Breatann (Fort of the Britons), capital of the kingdom of Strathclyde between the fourth and eleventh centuries. Legend says Merlin the Magician came here! The child Mary sailed from here to France, visited again during her brief personal reign in Scotland, and was trying to get here when the confederates cut her off at Langside. The castle held out for her until 1571.

Dunbar Castle: There is little left beside the harbour of the once great castle in East Lothian to which Bothwell abducted Mary. In December 1567 the Estates, the Scottish Parliament, ordered that the castle "be demolischit and cassin doune utterlie to the ground, and destroyit in sic wyse that na foundment thairof be occasioun to big thairupon in tyme cumming." (Big is Scots for build.)

Dundrennan Abbey: This Cistercian House founded by David I and Fergus, Lord of Galloway in 1142, was Mary's last place of rest in her native land. After the Reformation in 1560 the Lords of the Congregation had ordered Lord Herries to demolish the place, but he refused. After the last night in which she graced Scotland with her presence Mary left the abbey, South-east of Kirkcudbright, and embarked from Abbey Burn Foot. The name Port Mary is a reminder of her departure, and legend has it that a rock in the vicinity was the last part of Scotland to support her foot.

Dunfermline Abbey and Palace: The Fife town was once capital of Scotland, a designation which moved around with the monarch, but by the time Mary came here Edinburgh had acquired the title. An earlier Scottish Queen, St Margaret, who gave her name to Queen's Ferry on the Forth, founded the Benedictine abbey. There are remains to see, despite the destruction of the Reformation, but the site of the choir is now occupied by the modern parish church. King Robert Bruce is buried here. The abbey guest-house was uprated to a royal palace, and Charles I was born here.

Dunnottar Castle: The oldest part of this spectacular castle, dramatically perched above the sea near Stonehaven, is probably fourteenth century, but the site was in use long before, there being a record of a fort more than 1,300 years ago. There was a Pictish stronghold, and those interested in the legends of King Arthur will not be surprised to learn that Dunnottar is yet another supposed site of his Round Table. The Scottish Crown jewels were hidden from Cromwell here in 1651. Mary dropped by in 1562.

Earlshall: Mary is reputed to have visited when this sixteenth century baronial castle was a hunting lodge. It is beside RAF Leuchars in Fife. A seventeenth century painted ceiling bears the proverb: "A nice wyf and a back doore oft maketh a rich man poore."

EDINBURGH

Black Turnpike: The house Mary was first in-carcerated in after Carberry. Demolished in 1788 it stood in the Royal Mile, Edinburgh, to the west of the Tron Kirk, at the entrance to what is now Hunter Square. George Buchanan died here.

Craigmillar Castle, Here after the murder of Riccio, the French ambassador reported that Mary was "in a deep grief and sorrow." It was also at this grand castle 2½ miles South-east of old Edinburgh that the Craigmillar Band for the murder of Darnley was signed. The castle is a fascinating example of how an original fourteenth century tower was added to in succeeding centuries. It was burned by Hertford's army in 1544. In 1813 a human skeleton was found buried upright in the earth floor of the miserable dungeon. According to Sir Walter Scott this was evidence of a live burial.

Duddingston: this village, now part of Edinburgh, would have been on a route for Mary riding between Holyrood and Craigmillar. The historic Sheep's Heid Inn is reputed to have been visited by her.

Edinburgh Castle: For at least 1,400 years some structure has dominated the surrounding area from the volcanic plug known as Castle Rock. The oldest part of the present fortress is St Margaret's Chapel, commemorating the saintly Queen Margaret who died in 1093. The Half Moon Battery which is high on the left when the castle is viewed from the Esplanade (where the military tattoo takes place each August) was built on the ruins of David's Tower, much of which still exists beneath. The tower, dating from the time of King David II in the fourteenth century, was destroyed by cannon fire in 1573 when Mary's forces were obliged to abandon their brave five-year occupation. To the right of the Half Moon Battery is the Forewall Battery, which incorporates a stone plaque to the memory of Sir William Kirkcaldy of Grange "justly reputed to be one of the best soldiers and most accomplished cavaliers of his time, he held this castle for Queen Mary from May, 1568, to May, 1573, and after its honourable surrender suffered death for devotion to her cause on August 3, 1573." Above the Half Moon Battery is the Palace where Mary gave birth to the baby who later became "Jamie the Saxt", James VI. The date of that event, 1566, is carved in wood in the

Queen's bed-chamber and outside on a stone with the initials of Mary and Henry (Darnley). The Scottish Regalia of Crown, Sword and Sceptre is on display in a room of the Palace. Adjoining it on the castle's south side is the Great Hall, built for Mary's grandfather James IV and restored in the late nineteenth century at the expense of the publisher William Nelson after being used since 1650 as a barracks and then a hospital. Most of the walls which enclose the castle date from the seventeenth and eighteenth centuries. The Scottish National War Memorial opposite the Great Hall opened in 1927.

Holyrood: The Abbey adjoining the Palace of Holyroodhouse was founded in 1128 when King David I donated a gift of a piece of wood supposedly from the "true Cross" on which Christ was crucified, hence the name of the place, rood meaning cross. Another reason for the Holy Cross designation is told in the Holyrood Ordinale, a book written about 1450 and kept at the Palace. This claims that a stag knocked David from his horse when he was hunting and wounded the King's leg. A crucifix suddenly appeared between the stag's horns, which the King tried to grasp to save himself. He was left holding the cross and the stag made off. So the Abbey was founded in gratitude for the royal life being saved. A stag's head with a crucifix between the horns became the Holyrood crest, which gained worldwide circulation on the labels of the Robert Younger brewery, which used to offend royal visitors by wafting beery smells across to the nearby Palace until closure in the takeover mania of 1960.

Most of the Palace as it now stands dates from the rebuilding and extension which began in 1671 for Charles II. But the North-west tower, on the left when facing the Palace, is the original constructed beside the now ruined Abbey for James IV. This was the Holyroodhouse known to Mary, scene of conflict with John Knox and the murder of Riccio, as well as pleasant merry-making on happier occasions. In letters by Mary to Elizabeth Tudor from here the Palace is variably spelt "Halirudhous" and "Halyrudehous." The old tower is the final and most exciting part of the fascinating official tour of the Palace (not available when today's Queen Elizabeth and other representatives of the royal family are in residence.) As visitors walk through Lord Darnley's rooms and are then guided upstairs to Queen Mary's very own chambers it is possible to sense the mounting tension as they approach the scene of Riccio's violent end. The narrow private staircase up which the principal conspirators came has recently been revealed during renovation work, and a section has been left exposed to the public gaze. Unfortunately the original bed has gone from Mary's bed-chamber. The supper room from which Riccio was probably dragged is a surprisingly small room, adjoining a larger apartment where a metal plate on the floor shows where his body supposedly fell. (The mis-spelling of the name as "Rizzio" on this plate is one which has been repeated in countless books since a seventeenth century misprint!) Tourists used to be told that the metal was fitted to the floor because souvenir-hunters had been scraping off the stains of Riccio's blood, but unfortunately for that story during the rebuilding 300 years ago floors in the old tower were renewed when their levels were changed to match the new building alongside. However sections of original oak ceiling remain in the Queen's apartments including interesting carvings. A "catte" tapestry worked on by Mary is displayed.

John Knox's House: The belief that John Knox lived here in Edinburgh High Street saved this most photographed building from demolition in nineteenth century road-widening. Mary's goldsmith is said to have built it, and Knox did stay hereabouts.

Kirk o' Field: The scene of Darnley's murder has disappeared under the Georgian Old Quad of Edinburgh University, at the junction of South Bridge and South College Street.

Little France: This area of Edinburgh, beside the A68 Old Dalkeith Road, is so known because Mary's

French attendants stayed here when she was at nearby Craigmillar Castle.

Napier College in Colintón Road incorporates the stone tower of Merchiston Castle, where John Napier, inventor of logarithms, was born. There is a Queen Mary's Room, and the one-time garden was one of many reputed to have been graced by a tree planted by her.

Royal Mile: Collective name for road from Holyrood to the Castle, incorporating Abbey Strand, Canongate, High Street, Lawnmarket and Castlehill.

Scottish National Portrait Gallery and Royal Museum of Scotland: Well worth a visit the gallery is in the west end of the Victorian building in Queen Street which houses a section of the museum at the other end. The gallery displays representations of Mary, including the particularly fine bronze bust mentioned earlier. There are also paintings of the kings who preceded her, her son, her mother, and several of people linked to her story, among them "The Loyal Seton", George, fifth Lord Seton, master of Mary's household, painted by Frans Pourbos the elder when Seton visited Flanders with his sons in 1572. There is an engraving of Knox and a miniature of Bothwell.

Exhibits in the museum include relics of Mary and her time, among them a clarsach or Highland harp given as a gift by her to Beatrix Gardyne of Banchory, and a cast bronze piece of artillery with the arms of James, Earl of Arran, dated 1553 when he was governor of Scotland on the young Mary's behalf. The Maiden, the Scottish form of the guillotine, which was used to decapitate James Douglas, fourth Earl of Morton, among other public executions over many years, is dramatically displayed.

Edzell Castle: In 1562 on her way to fight the Gordons, Mary held a Privy Council here, north of Brechin. This sixteenth century castle was the seat of the family known as the "Lichtsome Lindsays". The walls of the superb formal garden display heraldic and symbolic carvings unique in Britain, of German inspiration.

Falkirk: Callendar House, in a park on the east side of the town, was a stopping place for Mary on several occasions.

Falkland Palace: As the name implies — "falcon land" — this was a favourite hunting centre for Stuart monarchs, and Mary was no exception. The thirteenth century castle of the Thane of Fife was here before the palace. Gruesome tales of violence are associated with the events that brought it to James II, who gave the charming wee town where the palace stands its royal burgh charter. Construction begun under James III was completed for James IV, who died at Flodden. Then James V, who was virtually the prisoner of his step father here as a youth, had French and Scottish masons give the palace its final appearance as what has been described as early Renaissance architecture without parallel in Britain. James V died here. In 1562 James Hamilton, Earl of Arran, who was said to have gone mad for love of Mary, attempted to abduct her from here to marry her. Interestingly, his accomplice was James Hepburn, Earl of Bothwell, who was later to put just such a plan into action on his own behalf at Dunbar. In 1887 — three hundredth anniversary of Mary's death — restoration of the palace began, eventually bringing it back to the condition of splendour in which it is cared for by the National Trust for Scotland. Catholic services are held in the Chapel Royal. Across the garden from the palace is the unique Royal Tennis Court, built in 1539 for James V, and still in use, like the other "real" tennis court constructed in 1625 at Hampton Court Palace.

Fordell Castle: Restored as his private residence by the Conservative MP Mr Nicholas Fairbairn QC this Fife castle was visited by Mary.

Glamis Castle: The childhood home of Queen Elizabeth, the Queen Mother, and birthplace of Princess Margaret in 1930, this castle has changed out of all recognition since Mary reached Glamis in 1562. Although dating from the fifteenth century most of it is seventeenth century, and there are more recent changes. The 21 feet high sundial in the grounds has 84 dials.

GLASGOW

Castlemilk: Little remains of this fifteenth century tower, in the housing estate of the same name. Mary may have stayed here the night before the Battle of Langside.

Haggs Castle: this late sixteenth century building houses a Glasgow museum with an exhibition about Mary Stuart.

Langside: The battle is commemorated by a monument erected in 1887 when the 300th aniversary of Mary's death was marked. The stone column, covered with representations of fleur-de-lys, roses and thistles, topped by a lion, stands in a roundabout at the junction of Langside Road and Battlefield Road.

Provand's Lordship: The oldest house in Glasgow, dating from 1471, it is believed to be where Mary visited Darnley. At 3 Castle Street, opposite Glasgow Cathedral, it is now a museum. The nearby Royal Infirmary is a reminder that this area has been associated with the care of the sick for more than 500 years, Provand's Lordship having been built for Andrew Muirhead, Bishop of Glasgow, as the manse for the Chapel and Hospital of St Nicholas.

Queen Mary's Seat: A large boulder in Cathkin Braes Park, this is on high ground commanding fine views for miles.

Glenluce Abbey: Cistercian house founded near Stranraer in 1192 by Roland, Earl of Galloway. Visited by Mary during her tour of the South-west in 1563.

Hailes Castle: A calling point for Mary on the way to Dunbar, this thirteenth century structure is in a beautifully peaceful setting beside the Tyne near East Linton.

Hallforest: In 1562 Mary visited this tower near Kintore, Aberdeenshire, where Robert the Bruce is thought to have had his hunting lodge.

Hamilton: Mary came here after escaping from Loch Leven. Cadzow Castle, where she stayed, was dismantled after Langside by the order of her brother Regent Moray. Cadzow white cattle are believed to be the survivors of wild cattle native to Scotland.

Hermitage Castle: Sir Walter Scott's favourite, this massive, grim fortress of mainly fourteenth and fifteenth century date, dominates Liddesdale, 12 miles south of Hawick. Here Mary visited Bothwell when he was injured.

Huntly Castle: A superb, baronial ruin this was the Strathbogie headquarters of the Gordons.

Inchmahome Priory: This Augustinian monastic house, founded in 1238, is on an island in the Lake of Menteith, reached by boat from Port of Menteith. There is only one other lake in Scotland — the artificial Pressmennan Lake in East Lothian. Robert the Bruce was here on three occasions, and Mary was taken to Inchmahome for safety when she was five. The monastic garden is known as Queen Mary's Bower, it being claimed she cultivated plants here.

Inverness: Mary's castle is long gone.

Jedburgh: This charming border town is a must for tourists arriving in Scotland by car from England on the A68. The house Mary lived in during her stay in 1566 has been excellently restored, after being in danger of damage by vibrations from traffic before road alterations a few years ago. A supposed death mask is among exhibits relating to Mary, but the 1950s style make-up applied to it looks gruesome! A visit to the Abbey is also strongly recommended.

Kenmure Castle: Another spot passed by Mary, at the head of Loch Ken, in New Galloway.

Leith: The historic King's Wark public house stands close to where Mary came ashore in 1561. Lamb's

House old people's centre may incorporate something of the house where Mary dined. The street name Tolbooth Wynd is a reminder of the Tolbooth built on Mary's orders, but demolished in 1819 in spite of the protests of Sir Walter Scott and others.

Lennoxlove: Home of the Duke of Hamilton and Brandon, hereditary keeper of Holyroodhouse, and Scotland's premier aristocrat, this property near Haddington is a fine example of how a basic castle keep was added to over many years to become a comfortable residence. In the oldest section there is a well of pure water, showing how useful such a resource was centuries ago when under siege. (Most other castle wells to be seen these days are stagnant or filled in, giving no real impression of the quality of water once available.) This was originally Lethington, home of Mary's Secretary of State Maitland, whose "politician's walk" is signposted in the grounds. There are exhibits from many aspects of British history over several centuries, including the map used by Hitler's deputy Rudolf Hess to fly to Scotland, and the casket which was said to have contained the incriminating letters produced to make Mary seem guilty of the murder of Darnley. Another supposed death mask of Mary is here, tastefully displayed without the embellishments of the one at Jedburgh. The change of name to Lennoxlove came on instructions left when she died in 1702 by the widow of the Duke of Lennox, and remains a memorial to her love for him. The Hamiltons came here because Hamilton Palace had to be demolished in 1919 due to underground coal workings. There is a herd of Cadzow cattle in the grounds.

Linlithgow Palace: The birthplace of Mary Stuart is one of the finest, most beautiful buildings in the care of the state. It stands on raised ground beside the fifteenth century church of St Michael overlooking Linlithgow Loch in an outstanding setting. The splendid royal structure became a ruin when the careless government soldiers who were billeted here in 1746 set fire to it in an effort to keep themselves warm. The

Romans may have had a fort here, and Edward I — "maleus Scotorum", the hammer of the Scots — had fortifications during his efforts to crush Scotland. A former castle gave way to the present palace, mainly fifteenth and sixteenth century. (Part of the north side was rebuilt between 1618 and 1620 after a collapse a few years earlier.) Mary rested here during her journeys to and from the west. Bonnie Prince Charlie was the last Stuart to reside here. In the midst of the grand courtyard is the King's Fountain of the 1530s. The palace contains the Great Hall where the Scottish Parliament met in 1585, the King's Hall which has an impressive hooded fireplace, and other fine architecture. Queen Margaret's Bower is at the top of a high tower. Here it was that Margaret Tudor sat for hours looking out for the return of her husband James IV from the Battle of Flodden. He never came.

Lochleven Castle: The island which bears Mary's gloomy prison is larger now than in her time, because the loch level was lowered by a new route being dug for the River Leven in the nineteenth century. The route to the fifteenth century tower is the same as in Mary's time, by boat from Kinross. Two small vessels, one named *"Mary Queen of Scots"* provide a shuttle service for tourists in the season.

Niddry Castle: This exciting sixteenth century keep where Mary rested after her escape from Loch Leven is being restored as a family residence, with public access under the auspices of the National Trust for Scotland. One-time home of Mary's friends the Setons it is near Winchburgh, and can be glimpsed from Edinburgh-Glasgow trains.

Queen's Hill: Traditionally Mary reigned in her horse and rested here, at the head of the Tarff valley, during her flight from Langside.

St Andrews Castle: This pleasing ruin by the sea is mostly sixteenth century, but there has been a castle on the site since about 1200. Cardinal David Beaton's murder here in 1546 was made a relatively easy matter for his Protestant attackers, because he was having the walls strengthened at the time and his assailants gained entry by mingling with the masons on their way to work. There is a fascinating bottle dungeon, hewn from solid rock. It is also interesting to inspect the mine and counter-mine, dating from the siege of 1546-7 when French and other Catholic forces hoped to get into the castle by tunnelling underneath. The Protestant defenders dug a counter-mine to break into the invading shaft.

Scone Palace: The place name is famous for the Stone of Destiny, stolen by the English in 1297. The present palace north of Perth is more recent than Mary's time, but some of her embroidery can be seen here.

Seton Collegiate Church: An important ecclesiastical monument, this church with its unusual tower is in an attractively peaceful spot off the A198 road. Some interesting stonework from the old house, long demolished, that stood nearby, is mounted on a wall in the grounds. Mary liked to visit this area, where the Seton family had their East Lothian residence.

Spynie Palace: This residence of the Bishops of Moray, two miles north of Elgin Cathedral, was allowed to fall into ruin after the death of the last bishop 300 years ago (bishops continued in the Kirk after the Reformation until controversy in the seventeenth century). Mary was here during her campaign against Huntly, and Bothwell came this way seeking support after Carberry.

Stirling Castle: This vital part of Scotland's defences was often held by English forces during the wars between the two countries. The hero William Wallace took it from Edward I and the Battle of Bannockburn was fought over control of the castle. Similar in many ways to Edinburgh Castle, standing on a basalt rock scoured into shape by the Ice Age, Stirling has been described as the brooch which clasps Highlands and Lowlands together. From the battlements it is easy to see why it had such strategic importance, the best route between southern and northern Scotland being via Stirling before the Forth was bridged on its wider sections further east in the modern era. Stirling's fifteenth century bridge across the Forth was partly rebuilt in 1749 after one arch had been blown up during the 1745 Jacobite rebellion. Among imposing buildings within the walls are the Great Hall, built by James III, the Palace of James V, and the Chapel Royal, built in 1594 by James VI. The Great Hall was badly damaged by alterations to make it suitable as a barracks, and restoration work now under way will take many years to complete. The rooms of the Palace are grouped round a courtyard known as "the Lion's Den" — because it was once used as a home for a royal pet lion. The Stirling Roundels, remarkable circular portraits carved in oak, are on display inside. They were taken down from a ceiling after one fell on a soldier in 1777. Mary's coronation was at Stirling Castle, and she returned several times as an adult. One night a candle set fire to the curtains of her bed, but she was awakened in time, although almost overcome by smoke.

Tantallon Castle: This imposing fourteenth century ruin stands atop a cliff east of North Berwick, opposite the Bass Rock, a seabird sanctuary. In November 1566 Mary visited Tantallon, a castle which featured in many important events in Scottish history.

Terregles: The house near Dumfries where Mary made up her mind to flee to England has been demolished, but the bed she slept in on an earlier occasion is to be seen at Traquair.

Traquair House: The oldest inhabited house in Scotland, this delightful place has sheltered royalty many times over a period of more than 800 years. It has also been a haven for the Catholic religion, a priest's room with a secret staircase being required after the Reformation. A Catholic Chapel is part of the property. It is said that the giant Bear Gates, which used to be the entrance, have remained closed since

Bonnie Prince Charlie left. An embroidered silk quilt on the Terregles bed was the work of Mary and her "Four Maries". Peter Maxwell Stuart, the laird, brews a famous ale.

Wemyss Castle: Darnley began his courtship of Mary here, at West Wemyss, Fife.

Whithorn Priory: In 1563 Mary visited the cathedral church founded in the twelfth century by Fergus, Lord of Galloway. The site, south of Newton Stewart, was the location around 400 AD of St Ninian's Candida Casa (White House), the first Christian Church in Scotland.

Whittingham Castle: Darnley's murder was plotted here, according to a tradition which says the conspirators made their plans under an ancient yew tree beside the fifteenth century tower, about two miles from East Linton (and convenient for Bothwell to come from Hailes Castle and Maitland of Lethington to come from the house now known as Lennoxlove).

THE END